MY CONTRACT IN EXILE

Life on the island of
St Helena before the airport came

Sue Fisher

Fane Publishing

Published by Fane Publishing

Copyright © Sue Fisher 2015
All rights reserved.

ISBN 978-0-9931547-0-6

Acknowledgements

Heartfelt thanks to Beth for her encouragement and help, and to Richard for his support and expertise.

Atlantic Ocean

Equator

Ascension

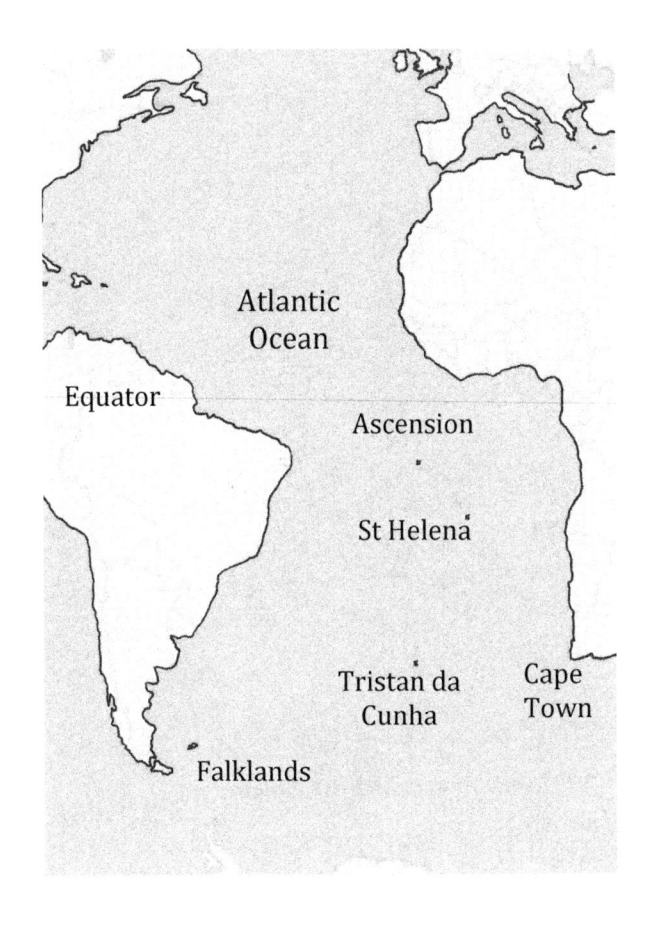

St Helena

Tristan da Cunha

Cape Town

Falklands

St Helena

Main settlements and roads
1 - Jamestown
2 - Longwood
3 - Half Tree Hollow
4 - St Paul's
5 - Levelwood
6 - Sandy Bay
7 - Blue Hill

Origin of the e-mails

It was so isolated that the British deemed it the most suitable place to exile Napoleon after he escaped from Elba. Two centuries later I was going there on contract and communications didn't seem to be very much better.

The second most remote inhabited island in the world, this volcanic dot of St Helena - it measures only 9 miles by 5 miles - lies in the middle of the South Atlantic. It is slightly closer to the African coast of Namibia than to the coast of Brazil, with the nearest land being Ascension Island 700 miles to the north.

St Helena lay undiscovered until 21st May 1502. Since then it has been fought over by the Portuguese, the Dutch and the English. It is now a British Overseas Territory and its people, the Saints, have full British citizenship.

There is no airport so the island is dependent on the one small Royal Mail Ship (RMS St Helena) and an oil tanker for bringing all goods and people to and from the island. When the RMS sails away from James Bay it will be 1 to 6 weeks before she is seen again depending on the schedule. If I were to retain my sanity and peace of mind on the island, I needed the lifeline provided by the exchange of e-mails.

Author of the e-mails

Previous life: I was a primary school teacher, wife of a Maths Adviser working for the British Government, and mother of three children. I met my husband in 1967 when we were both teaching in Uganda. Since then a large part of my life had been spent living, and working in education, in various parts of Africa with some time also in the Far East.

At the time of the e-mails: – I am still married and with three adult children, but looking to rediscover life after two years teaching in a state school in UK! My husband is again contracted, by the British government, to advise local maths teachers, train new ones and teach some A-level; this time in the middle of the South Atlantic. He also writes the occasional e-mail.

Recipients of the e-mails

Beth: Youngest child and my only daughter, born in Malawi. At the time of the first e-mails she has just graduated and embarks on a quest for a career. She is an incurable Afrophile and has a boyfriend, Olly. She encourages the daft and fanciful flights of imagination in her mother.

Jon: Younger son, with a Japanese wife, Chinatsu. At the beginning he is a qualified chartered accountant living in the UK with a newborn son. During my exile the family makes major changes in location and occupation. Jon encourages his mother to think independently and take the plunge into the unknown.

Tim: Elder son, born in Uganda. At the beginning he is living and working as a diplomat in Rwanda with his wife, Jo. Eventually he returns to the FCO London Office and Jo develops her career. Tim returns his mother to the sensible and realistic world, at the same time as sharing a love of and concern for the immense variety of peoples and places of this planet.

Rosemary: Assistant priest at my home church in UK, and a good friend.

Joy: A good friend and one who keeps me up to date with life in the village back home.

Letter of Introduction

Dear Reader

I thought I'd better write a letter to explain why there is no 'Contents' page. It would obviously be ridiculous to list over 120 e-mails so I had to come up with another idea. I thought of grouping them under subject headings such as:-

- Physical features and weather. (I studied geography)
- The presence or absence of sustenance. (Serious when looking at a veg. basket with just three potatoes, two onions and a tomato until the ship comes in)
- The radio. (That was fun)
- The choir experience. (Nothing quite like it)
- The comings and goings of the RMS. (Always significant)
- Everyday life in an island school. (I learned a great deal)
- Living with isolation. (Food for thought – did I mention food?)
- Island life at weekends. (There was plenty of it)
- Golf and the governor. (I got better over time, not sure about him)
- Church. (This really is better in small doses)

NB. The bishop referred to has since retired and there is now a different one on the island.)

Then I thought maybe just presenting them in chronological order, with the occasional break for 'Leave', and interspersing them with specialised e-mails to describe various distinctive aspects of life on this extraordinary island, is the best idea after all.

Just take things as they come. That's more or less what I did.

Yours faithfully,
Sue

PART ONE

Date: 27th November
To: Tim and Jo
Subject: Arrived at last!

I am here at last! I have arrived - and I am still recovering from a journey by train, car, plane, small ship and little boat.

My baggage was the regulation 52kg, pretty good as there was no pleading for extra allowance with the RAF. The flight from Brize Norton to Ascension Island was excellent and as we were travelling with a planeload of military guys heading for the Falklands the whole atmosphere was different from usual. Nobody made a fuss, everyone ate what they were given, there was no messing around with duty free and drinks first, and everyone did as they were told right down to the 'wait until the plane has come to a complete stop' and 'please clear up your rubbish and fold your blankets neatly'. Like lambs we were. We had individual hand held videos so I regressed and sat and watched Harry Potter, braving the scorn of the brawny, macho engineer next to me. Come to think of it he was probably watching it too.

Ascension Island is fantastic. We dropped down from 30 000 feet onto this tiny dot in the ocean. It is so barren for the most part, especially round the edges, presenting a strange landscape of lava, ash, cinder and honeycombed cliffs almost as if the volcano has just cooled down. Apparently the Americans tested the moon buggy on part of the lava flow. In contrast the central peak is covered in rich vegetation sustained by a mantle of mist and cloud. Then there are the forests of towering masts and intricate webs of cables, domes and dishes for all the communications including the good old BBC relay station we used to listen to years ago in Uganda.

I was in the one small hotel and met the other expats and some Saints who were also waiting for the ship. I had hired a car so was able to do some exploring - which didn't take long especially as I didn't bother with the American airbase!

We were taken out to the RMS St Helena by small launch and you'll never guess - I found I was in the cabin that Princess Anne had used on her visit to St Helena (celebrating the Quincentenary of the island's discovery). We saw her disembark and then be whisked off to the official residence high in the interior of Ascension. The princess was only on St Helena for a week, not destined for two years like me. I shared my cabin with a British judge who was coming out to do two weeks training of the island magistrates.

The voyage was superb with all facilities - a bar, mini-mini swimming pool (just bigger than a bathtub), games on deck during the day and entertainment in the evening, but everything on a small scale. I got rather wind and sun burnt but couldn't resist standing at the rails and just watching the sea and horizon, imagining how it must have been for people in sailing ships long ago. The evening meals were most enjoyable with the Captain and ship's doctor, the judge and her male colleague, a South African surgeon (coming to do 3 months locum here) and a couple of Saints - one of whom became very voluble and most amusing with a little lubrication!!

After two days, the dramatic cliffs of St Helena eventually loomed up out of the haze. The transfer from ship (anchored in James' Bay) to island was again in a little boat and there was Dad waiting for me among a throng of Saints on the waterfront. I joined him after the most minimal of formalities. I guess they can always find you - it's that small.

Date: 28th November
To: Beth
Subject: Settling in

Only five small boxes to go! Why do I do this? And what on earth possessed me to bring so many sheets and towels given that we are unlikely to have many visitors in the circumstances? Old habits die hard!

The house is fine and will do well enough for us for two years (as long as the cockroaches can be kept down to a tolerable level). It is a bit like a mobile home in look and construction but it is big and light and has been repainted (over all the cracks and repairs) and re-carpeted. There are new curtains in all the rooms too, but they are all 6" too short – measurements taken without allowance for frills and hems I suspect! There is a shower as well as a bath, which is great. The electric cooker was bought new for us and there is a reasonable fridge so I am all set up in my least favourite room. We have a lady who cleans all the compound houses but I am still landed with doing the cooking - oh for a Lasford or William to cook for me as in Africa!

The house is set in a big open compound, called Piccolo, with no separate gardens, and where we are situated is a bit like being in a goldfish bowl. The view is over to a couple of mountains/hills (depending if you are talking Kent or Canada) and we can see the sea from the sitting room window. However it has been so hazy since I have been here that we can't easily tell the difference between the sea and the sky.

St Helena feels much larger than Ascension. The terrain is far more convoluted with lots of ridges, valleys, minor peaks and vertical cliffs. We are up out of town on a sort of ridge in an area called Longwood just opposite Napoleon's last residence (if you don't count his tomb that is).

I must now drive down to the town - a truly hair-raising experience, as none of the roads is very wide so you have to use passing places and they have really tight hairpin bends. I will let you into the secrets of driving here another time.

By the way how did things go on Friday? Dad bet that you would lose your way back from Brize Norton but I said that you would have Olly with you so you would manage between you!

Choir practice at the cathedral tonight.

Date: 1st December
To: Jon and Chinatsu
Subject: Bar, beers and the bishop

Been here over a week now. We have been for a couple of walks in different parts of the island and it is an incredible mixture of scenery ranging from hills and very steep valleys reminiscent of Scotland to weird barren stark slopes and cliffs with rocks all shades of orange and brown - closer to Oman - and then the occasional corner which is covered with lush vegetation and a hint of Uganda. Almost everywhere of course you can see the sea or you know a view is just over the next rise.

I am beginning to meet some of the people, both Saints and expats. Thursday's choir practice at the cathedral (about the size of our home church) was interesting! – it being heavily conducted by the bishop (expat) who is anxious to get us ready for an innovation for St Helena - a Taize Service. My first impressions! - he is a very big man, very high church, knows everybody and likes to be at the centre of things. I next met him down at Donny's, the bar and eating-place down on the tiny waterfront, holding court and downing beers, with anyone who'd join him.

Donny's is where 'everyone' goes on a Friday night. Last night we met the bishop again at the St Andrew's dinner dance, where he was joining in with great gusto. This was an excellent occasion where Dad and I had a really good time. At the end we brought the new engineer home since she lives in the house next to ours.

Date: 2nd December
To: Jon
Subject: A small world in more sense than one.

Just remembered - I got chatting on the ship to the engineer I mentioned yesterday, who has come out to be one of the two top people running the Public Works Dept (PWD). It emerged that she remembers a particular occasion when she was working as a volunteer in South West Uganda some 10 years ago. On the day in question she and a young guy took out a dugout canoe on to Lake Bunyoni. The two of them were not overly efficient at propelling and steering this craft. Finally, when it was getting towards dusk with a storm brewing and they were getting nowhere fast, the anxious owner of the canoe decided to come out and rescue them. Yes, it would appear that the young guy was you Jon. I guess you remember it well. It is a small world is it not?

Date: 8th December
To: Beth
Subject: Exploring St Helena

On Friday I finished the Christmas post ready to take down to the town as the ship was going out this weekend. It's only 8th Dec - never been so efficient with this job before. The RMS was in the bay and Donny's was particularly full as everyone comes down to see and to meet people when the ship is in.

On Saturday we got up in a leisurely fashion and went down the hairy road into town yet again to see if the goodies from the boat had come into the shops, which they hadn't. But took the opportunity to stock up with crates and boxes of this and that while it was available. Then we set off for another part of the island to go for a walk.

It was about 40 minutes walking up an incline and most of it was quite steep, some on rock and some through trees but we had great views once at the summit of Great Stone Top. We were on a promontory and were able to look out to the vast expanse of ocean and then inland to the steep slopes of the valleys covered in pasture or trees. Suddenly there would be a cottage tucked in a fold or perched precariously on a slope and seemingly remote. But to be honest nowhere is really that far from somewhere else, though, as you have to drive so slowly, it may feel like it.

We went on another walk today and this was an official one so we had to rendezvous at Thompson's Wood at the other end of the island from here at 10:30. It took us 35 minutes to drive there since at no time did we do more than 25mph. Another great walk, more gentle for the most part but longer. We sat on the top of South West Point and looked out to sea. It looked very blue and then on either side there were rocks of many of different colours and very barren slopes down to the water's edge. Just starting on the way back in the car we met another car and they asked if we had seen the whales! Real whales? – lead me on! Apparently they hang about round here at this time every year.

Have you remembered Jon's birthday on Wednesday?

Date: 10th December
To: Jon
Subject: HAPPY BIRTHDAY

That special one when you are a real grown -up! I'm sorry we are not there for a party but hope that you have a good celebration on whatever day you have put aside for it. After all it is a family tradition to move birthdays around for convenience. According to Beth all you children will be getting together over the weekend, I'm sure you will have a great time.

I went, with Dad, to a school Christmas play today (juniors) and there are lights and decorations in the town but what with the warm weather, no school involvement on my part and none of you to prepare for it does feel rather strange - I keep on having to work out when Christmas is, if you see what I mean.

We have the yachts from the 'Cape Town to St Helena' race coming in all week which is rather fun and there are jollifications at the weekend. I have been working on using the video camera. Now I have to perfect that and work out how to put it all on the computer.

How is that grandson of ours? He must be holding his head up properly by now and hopefully sleeping for longer at a go.

Thinking of you and of one long, thin, bald, crying baby who turned out pretty well in the end!!!

Date: 11th December
To: Tim and Jo
Subject: Finding our feet

Welcome back to UK. It sounds as if it has been very cold so I guess it is a bit of a shock after Rwanda, but quite a nice change.

We have had very indifferent weather here since I came. Because we live up on the higher ground we are frequently shrouded in mist and you don't know what the weather is going to be when you get down into town. However we are only talking about whether one has a jumper on or not.

I am gradually getting to meet a few people but it seems to be taking time and as for the 'powers that be' they seem to be ignoring us more or less. That might be because one of the other advisers turned down an invitation from the governor a month or two ago, saying he 'hadn't got time for that sort of thing'! Not bothered about the governor particularly but others take their cue from him. Still we have been meeting some of the Saints especially those to do with the schools and church.

I hope to be able to do some work next term but can't fix up much now as everyone is involved in Christmas of course. We have had a great time going on different walks with the scenery changing round each corner. We were sitting on the top of a hill on the coast when we looked out to see the RMS steaming away across the ocean back to Ascension. You really do realise that now you are on your own.

The ship had just come up from Cape Town and yesterday everyone, including me, was rushing round in great glee buying up all the goodies. Our bags were bulging with green beans, oranges, apples, plums, apricots and even grapes. Otherwise there seems to be only potatoes, onions, carrots and cabbage - even tomatoes are in short supply. No doubt I'll get used to it but wouldn't want it for ever. Now I have to work out what we have to eat our way through and what I can freeze. Cooking and food - my favourites!!

Date: 16th December
To: Jon and Chinatsu
Subject: Helicopter overhead

What lovely photos, many thanks. Danny looks absolutely gorgeous. I thought our time over Christmas was going to be very thin but things seem to be improving although I shall sorely miss you all. An invitation to the Governor's 'Cocktails and Carols' has arrived so a visit to the famous Plantation House should be very interesting. I have been to three primary school nativity 'do's, there are carols down in the town to which our choir has to contribute and we have invited the people from the compound for a meal next Sunday - Christmas day is probably another compound affair and then a swim and picnic on Boxing Day.

I was walking over the golf course, which is just across the road from our compound, the other day and suddenly heard the sound of a helicopter which was odd as we are certainly too far from any land for one to fly here but there it was circling the golf course before going off round the island. Then I remembered that there is a South African Navy ship in the bay at the moment. It has come up in connection with the Commodore's Cup yacht race from Cape Town to St Helena. She was asked if she would also bring the supply of butane gas, which had been left on the quayside in Cape Town by the RMS, as it had been delivered too late!! So now we have gas but no diesel. The ship bringing the diesel had engine trouble and was delayed for 11 days but is due in tomorrow!! Each of our cars has half a tank. Echoes of Malawi and waiting days and days for fuel. This just reinforces the idea that this place is an odd mixture of Africa and Europe.

I do hope that you have a really good time in Japan.
PS Went for a walk yesterday after church, and climbed High Peak and could see exactly 10 yards. The mist had

blown in from the sea as it so frequently does and bingo - no view.

Date: 22nd December
To: Tim and Jo; Jon and Chinatsu; Beth
Subject: No mail for Christmas

RMS arrived on Friday but, alas, no mail. Apparently the RAF flight was late to Ascension Island and although the RMS delayed somewhat for the passengers it did not wait for post, not even the diplomatic bag. So there is no mail here for Christmas – very disappointing for everyone!

We hosted a lunch today for our neighbours on the estate: Bill and Mary, Bill doing things with blood in the hospital and finding it quiet here after a mission hospital in north-east Uganda; Viv who is sister tutor at the hospital and also doing training of nurses; Jill who is working for social services and has daughters Amelia year 9 and Laura post-grad on holiday from UK; Morag the engineer who runs the public works department. Mum seems to have spent a couple of days ransacking the shops for things and cooking. Needless to say, she produced an excellent meal and everyone seemed to enjoy themselves.

This evening we joined in and contributed to the island's ecumenical carol service led by the Salvation Army band and choir, with a novel nativity by their children. This was held on the steps of the courthouse in the main square, with a large Christmas tree and strings of coloured lights. Each of the main church choirs sang a carol and the congregation/audience had their chances to sing old favourites also. It went well and showed a good spirit of cooperation between the different groups.

Last Friday was cocktails and carols at Plantation House, the governor's residence. Everyone joined in the former, but only a self-selected minority the latter! He and his wife are spending Christmas on the RMS, as he is off to the meeting of all Governors in London early in the New Year.

Love to you all, hoping you have a great time in your various safe havens. Dad

Date: 28th December
To: Beth
Subject: Christmas Time - including golf

Well here I am sitting at our very posh new desk that Dad and I put together yesterday. - thank you for sending all the instructions.

I never imagined that I would really get a chance to do it but now I have - I started golf last Saturday! I went out with Morag and Jill, both of whom are only marginally better than me, and as no one was counting we were able go round without embarrassment. Mind you it took us the best part of 3 hours to do 9 holes. I learnt which way round the course to go, some of the vocabulary that one has to take on board and had a brief initiation into the etiquette involved. I suspect there is a whole minefield to negotiate in that area but we will see. I really enjoyed it apart from getting rather sunburnt.

I took myself for another round the next morning while Dad was doing his last day of work before Christmas. Do you know after paying our annual fee of £29 we don't have to pay any green fees ever! In the afternoon I went down into town to have tea with a Saint whom I had met on the ship. I found her house by dint of asking people in the street where she lived. It is that sort of community. She herself was well travelled as a surprising number of Saints are.

On Christmas Eve Dad and I went for a long walk with Morag and a young volunteer working for National

Trust. It was about 4 hours altogether and included some slightly tricky stuff round the edge of a steep rocky hillside and at the final point there was a vertical drop of cliff 400 feet down to the sea - not so good for my vertigo but fantastic for views. We stopped there for a bite of lunch. The contrasts in scenery are amazing from valleys with woods and rich vegetation through scrubby bush to bare rocks of many different hues and then the cliffs and the sea. We also started the walk by trying out a genuine 'bell' rock. I wonder if the size of the rock changes the note?

The evening consisted of some TV beamed in from South Africa and then midnight Mass.

2:00am bedtime meant we were not up early on Christmas Day but then we didn't have the patter of tiny feet (or big feet for that matter) to wake us up and get on with the presents. We had a leisurely morning, which felt really odd (bishop didn't think we needed a service on Christmas morning!) and we missed all of you but we got ourselves together and took a picnic and our walking gear for another trek. This time it was a steady though quite long, hike down through Lemon Valley (mind you nowadays there's not a lemon tree to be seen) to the rocky coast where there are the old ruins of a settlement where they kept released slaves in quarantine in times gone by. The thick, stone walls, the drip, drip of water and an atmosphere full of the ghosts of those poor souls, gave the place a strange feel.

We had a very brief swim (rather a big swell and lots of sea urchins being a deterrent) and ate a late lunch then started up the same path back. Somehow it was decidedly steeper, more dangerous on the slippery rocky bits and definitely much longer than the journey down – but then I always do 'down' better than 'up'. We arrived back to the car eventually but were an hour late for Christmas dinner with our neighbours and it took a little while for us to be forgiven. I think we were both happy but somewhat shattered so I was quite content to let someone else do the cooking! Mary and Bill have worked both in Zambia and Uganda so we had plenty in common. Finally got through to you on the phone after that. Apparently all the Saints phone their relatives working on Ascension and The Falklands, throughout Christmas Day.

Boxing day there was a ban on walking!! Well - more or less. We got up slowly and after lunch we drove to Rupert's Bay (where they bring the fuel in for the power station), with the idea of a gentle stroll round to the next bay and then a swim. The path proved to be very tricky and neither Dad nor I were in the mood for either a long walk, or one that consisted of climbing a narrow cliff path which fell away in places to nothing except a steep drop of a couple of hundred feet to the sea. It was very narrow and crumbly in other sections so we turned round and came back.

I hope you are looking after that cold and cough.
PS Did a very effective 'Christmas tree' out of branches 'appropriated' from the boundary vegetation of the compound. You would be impressed.

Date: 5th January 2003
To: Rosemary
Subject: Out and about in the holidays

I thought you might appreciate being spirited away to a tropical island for a few minutes. Actually it is not very tropical at all - warm and sometimes wet but not a palm tree or sandy beach in sight.

I wasn't sure how the holiday period would go - we being new here and this being the first time with none of the children with us but overall it wasn't bad at all.

Last Sunday we decided to take a holiday from the cathedral service and join the official walking party that Richard has been doing all his walks with, for their final trip and the picnic at the Environmental Centre afterwards. We climbed Diana's Peak which is the highest peak and more or less in the middle of the island (but it was too misty for really good views) and then went down a different route much of it through fields of flax (it used to be used for post office bags), now growing out of control, to the Centre. There, we had a so-called picnic meal. Whereas I had brought half a dozen sandwiches and a couple of cereal bars for the two of us the Saints had other ideas. I obviously have much to learn on this front. Out came pies, and chicken legs, bowls full of *plo* (rice and bacon and onion) and I'm not sure what else, salads (now where did they find stuff for those?), cakes, date pudding and much more and of course fizzy drinks and beer. They are a lovely set of people.

I met a young woman (Rebecca) whose dad had been on the same Teachers for East Africa course as Richard and I in Uganda, only a year later, and Rebecca had been born in Mengo Hospital just like our Tim. Small world.

On New Year's Eve we had a South African family of mother and her two sons for lunch and a climb up to Flagstaff - the nearest peak. She has no car, which makes things a little difficult as there is no public transport on the island, so we thought they might like a diversion in the holidays. Apparently they were very much city people but have adapted to life here very well.

At the New Year's 'do' in the Consulate Hotel in town in the evening, we were on a table with three Saints who are teachers, a couple who have come up from the Falklands for two weeks and who teach at the Army school in Port Stanley, and with a very lively chatty lady called Edith (a Saint) who was a teacher and then Chief Education officer on the island before she retired. The band was generally playing fairly oldie music, which was fine. Great fun was had by all and Richard and Edith each bought a bottle of champagne to help things along.

At about 00:45 we decided that we had better leave as we had promised to drop in to see our Scottish friends if their light was still on, which of course it was. As we got through the door we were offered steak pie! We finally got away and home to bed at 3:00 am. A definite need for a very quiet day the next day!

I went in to Richard's school on Friday morning to deliver something and he was reading the BBC British news bulletins on the internet. He sorely misses his newspapers – at least we got them when we lived in Africa, albeit a week or so late. We did not get our Christmas mail before Christmas and in fact are still waiting for it. The next visit by the RMS is this weekend when she comes back up from Cape Town so there will be some in the diplomatic bag then and the rest when she goes on to Ascension and returns. At least the ship's visit will mean some more fresh fruit and veg from South Africa. Schools start next week and I am expecting to be involved very soon so I guess the socialising will be reduced.

I think of you often, God bless,

Date: 8th January
To: Joy
Subject: Island personnel

A Happy New Year to you.

Thank you for all the news of village goings on. I am very fond of Doris she is such a character and we used to have good chats in the car when I gave her lifts. It is strange that her world is so different from mine. She has hardly travelled at all in all her years and yet she has had a very full life. I guess hers was made up of people whereas mine is mostly made up of places.

Which brings me to the people on this island. The Saints themselves, of whom there are about 3500, are very friendly and greet you everywhere although they are also reserved and I think it will take time to get beneath the surface. Thinking about it one can't blame them. After all expats come and go all the time and are usually on short contracts of 1 to 3 years. I remember working in Malaysia and it was the same there. After about three years we found that the local planters opened up to us and involved us more in their lives only for us to leave after four and a half years.

There are about 16 expats and they are a very mixed bunch and from a variety of places but especially UK and South Africa. First there are the Top Administration people (expats) – the governor, chief secretary and such like, whose attitudes to their position seem to be straight out of the 19th century; then there are the technical types (expats and Saints) for communications, shipping, roads, electricity and other utilities; the business sort (mostly Saints); and the professionals for health, law, education etc. (again a mixture though apart from education they are mostly expats). In education the Saints in the top jobs are excellent - very professional and hard working but unfortunately reducing in number as the younger generation are attracted to working overseas because of greater opportunities and more money. There are a good number of mixed marriages between Saints and those from off the island. The Saints are a wonderful collection in terms of colours and features - even more varied than Mandela's 'rainbow nation' which is not surprising as they are a distillation of many races drawn from a diverse background of countries and cultures including British, African, Malays, Chinese and Boer.

Then there are the church people. All the clerics I have seen, apart from the new American who has come in for the Baptists and an Anglican Brother, are well over 60 and are mostly expats. The bishop, who is based at the church we go to (technically a cathedral but smaller than St George's at home), is quite a strange chap – he's an important member of the island community; he loves his robes and finery; he is good at socialising but not so strong on the organising front; he is a bit blunt with our choir but he can put together a good sermon and can play the organ. He knows a large number of people on the island; he is a great raconteur and loves sci-fi movies. Apparently he comes under the Metropolitan of South Africa – whatever that means.

As for us we have settled in quite well but miss the friendly and welcoming missionary community that we have usually found when working abroad - but then this isn't Africa! I have just been asked if I will work at one of the four primary schools on the island so will be back in school next week when term starts. Excellent – should keep me busy!

We had a pleasant if unusual and quiet Christmas, and New Year was quite fun but I think I will be happy to get settled into some work now. Just as your temperatures are plummeting ours are rising steadily though since we live on higher ground we often find ourselves waking up in the cloud that has bumped into our dot as it raced across the ocean. If it is clear tomorrow morning I shall try and fit in a round of golf early before anyone else can see my efforts.

Look after yourself and please send our greetings to the people at church and the village.

Date: 8th January
To: Beth
Subject: New career?

Wonders will never cease - your beloved maternal parent surpassed herself on Sunday evening. She is now considering a career as soloist in oratorios and other sacred music, requests for appearances to be handled by her agent. The launching of this sparkling new career began by the singing of the first verse of 'Once in Royal...' by your parent as a solo in the cathedral (small church) at the back of the main aisle at the beginning of the carol/epiphany service, attended by a huge congregation (well about 50). The aforementioned agent said that the first few words were a little gravelly but that the rest was fine and clear and ended in perfect tune. This might be due to the fact that my knees were knocking so hard and I was so worried I'd run out of breath that I didn't actually think of the notes at all but just let it happen!

    I still don't know how I let myself in for that except that at choir practice the choir mistress asked me and I couldn't think of a valid reason why not (and the other sopranos are a couple of lovely but older ladies and past their prime). So solo career begun! The only compensation - just for once, despite being a special service, Radio St Helena weren't there.

    This afternoon I have to see the Education Officer for Primary as it seems there is some work for me in one of the primary schools. Actually the Head of this school is in the choir and mentioned something about it to me on Sunday.

    I'm glad that your New Year went well and that all your friends could get together. Now, as you say, down to the job searching. I guess it is a matter of balance but would it be worth considering the more mind numbing stuff if it actually brought in more cash? I truly am not nagging just interested and very sympathetic. I'm sure it was a good idea not to go straight on into the PGCE as you would never have been quite sure if you weren't just copying us.

    We had an e-mail from Jon from the airport in Japan and he seems to have had a really lovely time and sounded relaxed and happy. Tim appears generally full of beans and we had a nice e-mail from Jo in the holidays. So it would seem that all systems are going well at present.

Date: 18th January
To: Beth
Subject: Jobs and dolphins

It sounds as if you are having a frustrating time over work but I guess something will turn up. In the meantime I shall tell you about my job and other doings of this week. I don't expect you to be envious though, not since your Indonesian exploits!!

Firstly the new job. I am now working at St Paul's primary school (often called the country school as it is up in the hills inland) and I am assigned to the year 6 but am not responsible for it - great. This means that I have only a reasonable amount of preparation and limited marking and so should have time for a round of golf after school on Monday as well as the regular Saturday morning one, choir on Thursday and possibly badminton on Wednesday evening. It feels odd but I reckon I could get used to it.

Today we had a really lovely time. We went down to the waterfront with about 8 friends at around 9:30 am and boarded a fishing boat that Viv had arranged to take us to see the dolphins. About half an hour after we had set off there we were in their playground. This was just off Lemon Valley, which Dad and I had explored on Christmas Day. There are about 2-300 dolphins that are more or less permanently resident around the island and we were right in the middle of them. They were swimming by in waves - pod after pod, then they would leap high in the air as if trying to show off to us. We watched for about an hour as we could see them playing around almost as far as the eye could see in all directions.

Eventually we dragged ourselves away and carried on along the coast identifying several of the valleys that were the locations for the walks Dad did before I came and some I have done since. Almost all the coast is made up of high cliffs with multi-coloured layers of rocks, every now and then cut by steep, narrow valleys reaching for the sea. Frequently these valleys have some sort of fortification wall built across them (often only a few hundred feet wide). These were for defence by the British to deter would-be invasions from the Dutch and Portuguese! They each wanted to grab the island as their staging post on the route down the Atlantic and round the Cape.

We entered a more protected cove and took the opportunity to dive into the sea off the boat as landing would have been too difficult. The beautiful clear, deep blue water was surprisingly warm considering that this was the South Atlantic. We had lunch on the boat and then made our way gently back to Jamestown. It was fascinating putting everything in its place from off shore as one can get very muddled with direction and distance when driving up, down and round the tortuous roads of the island. I was thinking that it was the first time we had left our 9 mile by 5 mile dot of rock for many weeks but it has not seemed claustrophobic or restricting, at least not in the everyday sense.

Better go to bed before I fall asleep dreaming of dolphins.

Date: 26th January
To: Beth
Subject: Helloooooo!

Hellooooooooo!

I assume that you are writing something at the same time as I am writing this but it is unusual not to hear from you for over a week. Here is our news of our week at the centre of the world. It has been good and I am thoroughly enjoying the schoolwork mostly because I am not responsible for too much and the preparation is reasonable. If I could fit the work into 4 days it would be even better.

I had the novel experience on Friday of going down to the school staff room to collect my salary in cash in a little brown envelope along with all the other staff. I remember my Gambian science teachers doing that in the middle of a workshop I was leading for them. They became very anxious because I was determined to finish something first!! I hadn't realised that – if they were late - the government van would drive away without paying them and they would have to travel all the way to Banjul to get their money and that could well take them a week.

Bank accounts are not really the thing here for most people. There isn't a proper bank as we know it and certainly no cash points. We have some complicated system through the government office to get our money as Dad's salary is paid in UK. Getting cash as I do, though it is so little, is actually very useful.

Friday night I left my school, went to pick up Dad and carried on down Ladder Hill into town where we had a swim for the first time, in the lovely pool they have down on the waterfront. The water was beautifully warm and the air just pleasant - not too hot. Later at Donny's Bar at the other end of the waterfront, about 500 yards away, we joined the TGIF crowd and over an excellent T-bone steak (none of the CJD stuff here) we had a good chat with a few others including the bishop. He has spent many years in the Zulu areas of South Africa and had some good tales to tell.

Last night we went off to the Burn's Night Supper. The bishop, a full-blooded Anglo-Saxon, is the Chief but there were a couple of Glaswegians who gave the speeches, and the haggis came in on the RMS a week or two ago! It was a very a pleasant evening and we both ate too much.

I nearly forgot - I did a par 4 hole in 4 yesterday and felt very pleased with myself. I promptly followed it with a disastrous 12 at the next hole but there does seem to be some hope for me at least.

Date: 11th February
To: Jon and Chinatsu
Subject: A simple life

Fantastic photos - many thanks. They really are super and I love the ones where Dan is smiling, he looks really lively.

I'm glad the visit went well and that you managed to give Chinatsu's mother a good glimpse of your life in UK. She obviously felt confident enough to relax so should feel quite refreshed and possibly very slightly envious on her return to Japan!! Glad also that you were able to make some more contacts in the quest for secondment to Japan. All that sort of thing appears so complicated these days, with so many factors involved and nothing quite what it seems.

Life here gives the impression of being very simple in comparison. Mind you one does have to watch what one says to whom at any time, as everyone is related or connected in some way - treacherous ground for the outsider. Even parent/teacher meetings can be fraught with difficulties. Safest to say everyone is 'trying'!

I am hoping to send a couple of photos this week or weekend including one of us all togged up in our choir robes. I am also busy composing one of my insights into life here, this time about driving. Then there's 'glorious food or lack of it' and 'when the ship comes in', actually these last two are somewhat related.

Must go as this is mid week and we cannot be sure that Morag's darned cockerel has been locked up for the night so we could be woken at 6 am!

To: Tim and Jo; Jon and Chinatsu; Beth
Subject: A special on History

'A history lesson'
Dearly beloved but sadly ignorant children,

Before we go any further I believe I have to right a wrong. I realise that not one of you dearest offspring has the first idea about European history since we always seemed to up sticks and go off to distant parts of the world just after you'd done the Vikings. Therefore I feel it incumbent upon me to fill in the gap at least as far as Napoleon is concerned. After all he is the only reason most people have ever heard of St Helena.

Crash course on Napoleon and Longwood.
Napoleon was born in Corsica in 1769, a son of a minor noble family of Italian ancestry. He joined the army. He was a general by 1794. He married the famous Josephine in 1796 and eventually ruled France as Consul from 1799 and was proclaimed emperor in 1804. Seemed to rule half of Europe. He was a constant pain and worry for England. He led a campaign against Russia and reached Moscow but had to retreat in 1812 – you know the music! More ups and downs and a spell exiled on Elba from which he escaped. Then Wellington and the Allied armies finally defeated him at the Battle of Waterloo in 1815 – you must have heard of that. Napoleon was eventually taken prisoner and it was decided that he be exiled on the remote island of St Helena where he eventually died! That really is rather condensed but you get the picture – dozens of books about him if you want more. Now the St Helena bit.

Napoleon arrived at St Helena on board HMS Northumberland on 15th October 1815. Longwood house had been chosen as the most suitable place to put him but it required alterations and extensions. It had originally been built as a rectangular barn and then in 1787 one of the governors converted it into a summer residence. Apparently Napoleon rode with Admiral Cockburn and General Bertrand, the Grand Marshal of the exiled court, to inspect it. The French were not impressed. General Bertrand described it as a few dark rooms with low ceilings, and the garden as bare and windswept, without shade or water. In the book 'Napoleonic sites on St Helena Island' it says an eyewitness of Napoleon's exile, Dr John Stokoe, Naval Surgeon, described Longwood as follows: "Longwood alone, on a plateau 1800 feet above the sea, bears the full brunt of the south easterly gales. For five years and a half Napoleon lived in a perpetual whirlwind. The persistency of the trade winds is not their only drawback. They carry with them vapour which passes continually over Longwood in the form of clouds, and falls either in the form of tropical showers, or condenses at evening into thick fogs which rest on the ground..."

This, I might say, is the same Longwood where we live - our house being less than 5 minutes from Napoleon's place. It is definitely damp and windy. We have to have an electric light bulb on permanently in each wardrobe to try and stave off the damp and protect our clothes and shoes. I gather in his day the walls literally ran with moisture almost all the time!

..the most detestable spot in the universe... I hate this Longwood, (Napoleon)

While the restoration was being carried out he had a few months in a place called The Briars. It is in Briars Valley near the Heart Shaped Waterfall and belonged to a chap called William Balcombe. Napoleon was very fond of the summer pavilion and stayed in that and it was definitely in a more pleasant part of the island.

Napoleon's life on the island was very bizarre and there are numerous stories about what went on and about the less than harmonious relationship with the Lieutenant Governor, Sir Hudson Lowe. Numerous conspiracy theories exist about how Napoleon was poisoned with arsenic by various people but the reality would appear to be less juicy I'm afraid. Scientists think that, though there was arsenic in the green pigment of the wallpaper and as a result of the humidity, mould and fires in the hearth, this probably became airborne (hence trace elements in his hair), he did not die of arsenic poisoning but of stomach cancer.

He was buried in the Vale of Geraniums just north of Hutt's Gate. It is lovely there – very quiet and beautiful. Yet again there was controversy as the French and English could not agree as to what should be written on the tomb so the French decided to leave it blank! But of course his body isn't there any more. It was exhumed in 1840 and taken back to France and buried under the dome of Les Invalides in Paris.
Longwood became a cattle pen and a pigsty before being rescued by the French.

It is quite difficult to imagine it in some ways because it is so different now. Longwood Old House, gardens and the land comprising the Tomb Estate are now a French domain. There is a French Consul whose job it is to look after the house and other sites and to make them available to visitors. The grounds are now beautiful and there are a number of quite big trees around the garden.

We tagged on to the end of a party of tourists from a visiting ship and the tour was fascinating. There is his bed (a kind of camp bed) and his deep iron bath in which he would spend hours apparently. There is a death mask and various bits and pieces associated with him. One thing that made him very human to me is that there are two peep-holes that Napoleon himself cut into the louvred shutters with his penknife, so that he could spy on the sentries and watch the comings and goings of the English!

It would seem that Napoleon's coming to the island was a very good thing as the population almost doubled with the arrival of the English garrison involved in guarding him and making sure no one got near to help him escape. Then there was the surprisingly large retinue of French people. This meant that plenty of money was spent on the island and

there was demand for everyday things. Mind you this was a bit tough on the island's resources and much as today a great deal had to be shipped in! It was rather catastrophic when he died and they all went away.
End of history lesson.

Date: 4th March
To: Tim and Jo
Subject: Impending leave

Leave plans for September so far - this will be our first leave away from the island in the two years, and much shorter than we would have liked because of the RMS schedule. We have booked a lovely cottage near Bala and have confirmed the week in Bath with you all joining us. This will be after a visit to Kent and a stop over at Jon and Chinatsu's for Danny's birthday.

We know that we're lucky to be seeing you at all. May we visit you in South America should you get that posting, on our way home from here in summer/autumn 2004, or 2005 if we have an extension? People here think that Ascension Island, as an American base, will close to civilian traffic in the event of war in Iraq. I'm glad we planned the southern route home.

Date: 9th March
To: Rosemary
Subject: Revolution brewing

Two Fridays ago in the evening there was a definite buzz in town when we arrived. The local newspaper was just out with the announcement that the planning permission for some inward investment which had been granted had now been overturned by the St Helena Government i.e.

governor and co. and as far as one could tell it was not done very tactfully. Now tempers were boiling over and there were loud calls for the resignation of the governor and the Chief Secretary (who had just nipped away on leave). An angry meeting was held on the following Monday night and there was a sign outside some building saying 'out with the old and in with the new'. A protest march was planned, a petition and goodness knows what else. Apparently there were about 100 on the march on Saturday with all sorts of banners (incitement to violence not allowed) and about 400 in the main square for the speeches. It was covered in detail on the local radio.

Richard and I were on the golf course as was the Governor! 'Expats keep heads down and mouths closed' is what we learnt in Africa! Who would have thought it in this little island - take a back seat Sadaam. This whole saga has been rumbling on for months if not years and is connected with the possible airport.

Of almost equal cataclysmic importance to me is the fact that we found a large rat running round our bedroom when we came in from watching the Pancake races and eating curry and rice in town. After some frantic and unseemly efforts to attack it with a broom we decided to make a 'rat run' with bits of cardboard and furniture so that when it was chased from the bedroom it had nowhere to go but out! Next step - rat-traps in the loft. These dear creatures' ancestors came off the sailing ships when St Helena was such an important watering hole for ships trading between Europe and the East.

Yesterday Richard and I put on our climbing boots and went on a hike up on to the ridge to Diana's Peak (about 800m) again. It is the only point from which one can see almost the entire island and nearly 360° view of the sea. As we sat up there and looked out over the valleys and ridges, the flax, tree ferns, the lush forests and all the little houses dotted about here and there, it was brought home to me how very small the island is and how remote. Then I recognised the house of a young couple we have met several times on the organised hikes and whose two young children come to my school. The wife originally came as a VSO and has been on the island for 10 years and is quite happy to remain here as part of the community for the rest of her life.

Three and a half thousand is more than many country communities in UK and the scenery is beautiful but to live here permanently - I don't think I could do it. No chance to get away from it all, nip up to London on a whim, down to Bristol to see Beth, across the channel to explore a new area of France for a weekend, visit Tim and Jo, even go on a short contract somewhere. Maybe it is knowing that I could do that if I wanted to, rather than actually needing to do it, that is the important bit!!

This is not to say that I am feeling claustrophobic here at the moment, after all I've only been here 4 months and there is still much to learn that is new. Last week we went to the Ash Wednesday service and I was still wondering what I should give up (there is not much point doing my usual sweets and chocolate which I love, as we don't get many here) when I suddenly realised I could give up getting frustrated with the bishop for a whole six weeks and think positive thoughts all the way to Easter. A far more constructive way to proceed I've decided.

I'd better stop and make sure that my three children get their weekly dose of e-mail quality time with their mother. Daniel has just cut his first tooth so I had better respond. What a long time ago since our children were at that stage isn't it?

Date: 12th March
To: Beth
Subject: The social whirl

Just recovering from a couple of late nights. I found myself at the golf club social on Friday night! Jon would have a fit with his socialist point of view but in fact it is not as bad as it sounds. The whole reason for going was to show willing and get to know one or two more Saints as they are the ones who like these socials and they certainly don't fit in the category one usually thinks of for golf clubs. Dad was still recovering from the tummy bug so I had a couple of drinks, shouted a conversation through the country and western music and was dragged by Mary on to the floor for a couple of dances! Then having spoken to all of two Saints (they all stand at the bar or sit solemnly round the outside edge of the room like in Africa) I bowed out and went home. I'm glad I did it though.

Last night was an invitation to dinner with the Governor. Plantation House is quite impressive having been finished around 1785 and so in the old imposing pre-colonial style with big rooms, high ceilings, heavy drapes and antique furniture it definitely felt like moving through a minor stately home, though probably with fewer rooms. The occasion was very informal and there were only eight guests. The conversation at dinner was good and I enjoyed an intelligent chat with David (Governor). The lady of the house was in a very genial mood. We had a bit of an insight into the royal visit by Princess Anne, from their point of view too! Generally a successful evening though I could have dressed down a bit - it is so difficult to tell - hey ho.

As for other news I managed to get my lowest score so far at golf yesterday morning when I went out with Dad. That is another achievement of note - getting Dad out anywhere, let alone on a golf course, by 9:30am on a Saturday. In fact it has been great to have golf because there is precious little else and although the walks are enjoyable it is a bit more of a major operation and one certainly couldn't do it after work.

There are one or two short walks round the Longwood area but not very exciting. Dad is doing a big one today with the Conservation Club. It is a grade 9/10 walk (max 10) and involves a knife edge, so I am giving it a miss as you know I'm liable to get a touch of vertigo with 300 foot cliffs and this might be a bit inconvenient. I have been following progress through binoculars from our bungalow as this little string of ants climb the Barn, a huge solid lump that has sheer drops to the sea.

We seem to be heading for another Taize service soon and we will be having a concert type Songs of Praise in the cathedral, with the Ladies' Orchestra.

Date: 9th April
To: Beth
Subject: Frogs!

There's no getting away from it. I am a mass murderer - Sue Frog-Slayer Fisher that's me! On the way to choir practice last night through really torrential rain, a thousand tiny frogs seemed to rise up all along the roads and banks into my headlights and under my wheels. I actually tried to avoid one - not a good idea. On the way home and still raining I had another look and some seemed more like grasshoppers this time. OK so I'm a Cruel Cricket Crusher - then again I'm sure I saw another frog so perhaps we are being visited by the ten plagues of Egypt (I bet not every angel is good at geography) - blood and boils next. That's not as far fetched as you might think if you could see the colour of the water coming through our taps just recently!! The actual choir rehearsal was an experience as well.

Date: 9th April
To: Beth
Subject: Business

Dad and I have given due thought and discussion to the question of putting Olly as a named driver on the car and I am sorry to disappoint you my love, but have come to the conclusion that it would not be a good idea mostly because of the insurance. We don't doubt Olly's competence but he really is in just the wrong category - male, under 25 and a student - everything wrong except of course he is a lovely chap.

We hope you have a good trip anyway. Will be in touch again but thought you'd like to know so that you can plan. Must go and see if Saddam has been caught yet - isn't it weird watching blow by blow or do you get less of it not being tied to BBC World radio?

Date: 19th April
To: Tim and Jo
Subject: The island Ladies' Orchestra and Holy Week experiences!

Many thanks for your last long and interesting e-mail. Mind you I was a bit envious of the fact that you have the opportunity to have long serious discussions with anyone albeit heated ones. The job sounds fascinating Jo, when do you hear one way or the other?

On the church front I - (Dad has been ill with a chest infection and stomach upset) have had some - shall we put it - 'interesting' experiences. It started with The Palm Sunday service which was supposed to involve a procession all round the church but since it was pouring with rain and had been doing so since the night before we did a quicky carrying our yard long palms down the aisle whilst juggling hymn books, glasses, collection and singing, thus putting all and sundry at risk from having an eye gouged out. Palm crosses were given out and the bishop even stuck one in the crucifix, which I found just a little odd! The rest went much as usual.

Then in the early evening there was the Songs of Praise concert/service (nobody ever really sorted out what it was) organised by the island's Ladies' Orchestra. At the previous week's rehearsal some rather interesting aspects were revealed:
1) All the music was full of celebrations of Easter Day and we were doing it on Palm Sunday, the beginning of Holy Week - organisation and forward planning not brilliant - but you can't fault the bishop on being cheerful and friendly!
2) All this music came out of a chorus book (equivalent to Mission Praise only less musical.)
3) We solved the problem of the faintly difficult bits of the tricky one - we didn't do them.
4) The ladies' orchestra consists of one violin, one piano accordion, two guitars, three flutes, four recorders, one euphonium, two clarinets and a keyboard.
5) Half the choir was in the orchestra and most of the others didn't come to the practice.

It was all right on the night! In fact it went quite well and we were joined by a Salvation Army singing group, another from the Seventh Day Adventists, solos by the Baptist minister and Brother Christopher. There was also a choir of children from the school at which I teach. The congregation had a good sing. It was all being recorded by Radio St Helena, ready for broadcast on Easter Sunday (so maybe just as well about the hymns).

Tuesday – Baptist bible study down in town - the mandatory 45mins of chorus singing with guitar, accordion and mandolin, half an hour of very basic bible study on justification and sanctification and a further 45mins on eats, tea and chat!

Wednesday – Brother Chris was ordained deacon. An 'experience' full of clouds of incense, bells, a bevy of clergy including the Roman Catholic priest, a positive rainbow of robes, two hours of ceremony and the Eucharist service in full mass style. I found it somewhat disconcerting and thought provoking to find Brother Christopher lying prostrate in the aisle, directly between our choir stalls, as part of the ceremony.

Thursday's stripping of the altar took things to the extreme and the entire sanctuary and chancel were divested of anything that wasn't nailed down - Pickfords furniture removal was no competition - rather lost its simplicity and symbolism for me but the bishop made an efficient foreman.

Good Friday – the folk at the cathedral were going to have communion and hours of unspecified things so I decided to go to our local church for the hour (Dad still being unwell)

Heyho - we should have a good sing on Sunday (although the first Easter service and lighting of the Easter candle is early on Saturday evening!! - very muddling). In the evening we are having half a dozen or more people in for supper. I am cooking the turkey we bought for Christmas but didn't use (it was waiting for the next special occasion), and doing salads and two of my friends offered to do puddings - great. Although it is Dad's birthday we are not making that an issue.

Well Happy Easter to you both,

Date: 22nd April
To: Beth
Subject: Dad's birthday supper

Many thanks for your phone call to Dad - it cheered him up no end. He has been feeling very poorly for the last week. However he felt much better when we had friends in on Sunday.

Luckily we had only asked our better known friends since I was somewhat delayed by a light bulb bursting in the sitting room about an hour before the meal, as I was trying to change it. One thing lead to another and instead of being well organised and ahead I was rushing. I heard a car pull up so stuck something under the grill, and hurried through to the bedroom to change then of course I could smell burning so raced through the assembled crowd saying 'pretend I'm not here ' and dashed in to the kitchen but it was really too late for that particular dish.

Two of the ladies had brought a dessert so at least I didn't have that to worry about. The rest of the food was actually very good especially the tinned ratatouille! Why do I do these things when I haven't got you and Jon to rescue me? We settled for a good natter and everything went very happily with Dad doing remarkably well. It ended quite early, partly because one of the guests was well lubricated and suddenly stood up in the middle of someone else talking and announced 'time to go' - very subtle.

At this moment I think it is quite appropriate to send you my latest special piece, which is on food. There is more to add about the fact that for the islanders eating is an important pastime and there are several special dishes specific to the island, but this will do for the moment.

To: Tim and Jo; Jon and Chinatsu; Beth
Subject: Another special

'Kiwi fruit and tomatoes, black pudding and bulls' eyes'

Reluctantly I turn to the topic of food. There is no doubt the ship's arrival is always eagerly awaited and this visit was a good one as far as fresh food went. Our fridge is now bulging with grapes, peaches, pears and apples besides the first green peppers and lemons in three months!! That will have to keep us going for a good time now as the ship has just set off for UK and even when she comes back (in a month's time) she will have to go off to Cape Town before we see any fresh fruit again.

The first impression is that there is nothing on St Helena but potatoes, carrots, onions and cabbage to go with fresh pork or tuna. Even those cannot be guaranteed since the island more or less ran out of onions just recently and last year, so the story goes, there were no potatoes with a subsequent run on rice and pasta till they disappeared as well. However one begins to realise that the limited variety in the shops bears no relation to the real state of affairs on the island and that a great deal never reaches the shops at all. Exchange is the name of the game.

The school staff room sometimes resembles an amalgamation of a WI bring and buy and a farmers' market. A whole arm of bananas is put in the middle of the table from which anyone can help themselves, mysterious packets of homemade goodies (later found to be chunks of the local black pudding) appear in people's usual places. Children are sent to deliver a dozen eggs to a classroom and return with a bag of plums or medlars. A jar of honey is quietly offered to the favoured few. Squab lobsters and the white fish locally known as 'bulls' eyes', mean that the staffroom fridge is bulging with slippery plastic bags. Being an expat (especially in a house with no garden) is a considerable disadvantage – what good is our money in a world of exchange? I don't know if it is divine providence but the bishop mentioned the other day - down at Donny's, when he was demolishing a large plate of chips – that in his garden there were tomatoes, cucumbers, celery, pineapples, mangoes, lettuces, peaches - I forget the rest I was slavering so much. Should he be reminded about breaking fast together and taking care of widows and orphans and surely it says somewhere don't forget gasping parishioners?

There is plenty of pork and of course some lovely fresh tuna and a fish with the delightful name of wahoo. A fish van trundles round the island with wahoo and tuna steaks still wriggling in their locally wrapped polystyrene and plastic packets although one has to be on the bush telegraph to know when it is coming. A member of staff's father-in-law is a fisherman and sent some squab lobsters into school one week so we had a great meal of 'lobster in whisky and cream' a la Delia Smith – though the squat lobster was a local substitute, the parsley was dried, the cream was whipping cream left over from Christmas (no fresh here) and the spices were a creative approximation! Still the whisky was real.

However there are times and seasons when there is little variety on offer and staff begin to watch with unnatural interest the contents of each other's lunch boxes! An envious enquiry is made, 'My, where did you get that kiwi fruit?' to which the culprit replies, 'I've been saving it right from when the last ship came in! Anyway I saw you with a tomato yesterday!' Dinner parties can set off a conflict in a proud hostess' breast between showing off that she can produce such delicacies in a time of scarcity, and having to share with 6 or 8 what might have been secretly enjoyed by just two! I have no such problems since I am not a good enough or interested enough cook to care for my reputation, I just struggle with my conscience as to whether my husband would be better off if I ate his portion of avocado as well.

Date: 26th April
To: Joy
Subject: My birthday

Many thanks for your greetings, particularly appreciated as the post is so bad that there was nothing in the way of cards and so on. For my birthday we went in to town in the morning for me to collect my pay packet at the education office. Did I tell you that I am now the science teacher for the school? That means I teach science throughout the school and only in half classes at that - what a luxury. It is the British curriculum slightly adapted. I also have a well-equipped lab to do it in. This is because it is a left over from when the school had pupils up to 14 years. Richard is also enjoying being a Maths adviser to both primary and secondary and doing some A-level teaching which gives him freedom to plan and put the priorities where he wants to. He works from home, in the secondary school and at the Education Centre. He will also soon start training some student teachers.

The town was positively buzzing and full of people as there was a huge cruise ship anchored off shore and hundreds of tourists had come on to the island to view the locals and visit the sites associated with Napoleon. Many islanders get one-day taxi licences for these visits as there is no public transport for visitors to get around and it is a good way for local people to make money. The museum and its shop also do well. There is a lovely little gift shop in the basement below the main hotel selling local lace, paintings, woodcarvings and prints of the island.

We have done quite well for ships this year as cruise liners have avoided the Mediterranean because of the Iraq war and so looked for somewhere else to go. Occasionally the swell is so bad that visitors cannot land because the ships will not use the local landing craft only their own, and inevitably their sailors are more nervous and less experienced with the local conditions and so don't attempt it. Then there is great disappointment and loss of revenue all round.

After lunch at one of the two coffee shops, we set off to Sandy Bay on the opposite side of the island i.e. 4 miles away! This area is in fact very different from Jamestown and I am rather taken with it. The road is extremely narrow and winding and first works its way down an incredibly green valley thick with flax, bananas, eucalyptus trees, forests of trees I don't know and a good selection of flowering plants (botany never was my strong point). Once through this, the vegetation begins to thin as you follow the way to the coast. The road gets even steeper and the tight, steep, hairpin bends make driving quite fun. The vegetation disappears altogether and you are left with rugged, barren cliffs and amazing outcrops of rocks all of different colours.

Finally we parked the car and walked the last couple of hundred yards to the fortifications and the beach. There are the remains of several batteries and a defence wall to ward off any invaders and some indications of the barracks that must have held a good number of soldiers. I wonder what they thought of their posting in the 18th century? The sea was fairly calm and you could actually smell it. It is amazing how, although we are surrounded by it and it is never far away, we generally aren't aware of either salt or the smell of the sea. We had a good explore and a bit of a picnic before the equally exciting drive home!

Date: 17th May
To: Beth
Subject: Golfing depression

Why on earth does anyone play golf? I haven't done so well just recently. It must be the fact that there are magnificent views of the highest peak covered in flax and tree ferns in one direction, barren cliffs and jagged hill tops towards the coast, a steep tree covered valley into which your ball could disappear if you were good enough and then miles of ocean. How am I supposed to concentrate on hitting a little white golf ball! I was so fed up after my efforts the other morning that I decided to go and dig up some weeds in the garden of an empty house and spend some energy planting a sort of boundary to pretend we have a private patch of grass. Now I have blisters and so probably won't be able to play my regular game on Saturday morning after all.

Saturday - I think perhaps I ought to give golf a break, as I seem to be going downhill instead of improving. I wish we had a driving range here so I could whack 100 balls at a session and see if I can work out how to do it. However I have taken up drawing again and have done one of The Barn with which I am quite pleased, and another of a lily. This afternoon I stuck my golf bag in the middle of the room and drew that - I reckoned I'd have more success drawing it than playing with it. I think I was right!

I have written a special piece about the weather in this weird place of ours. I just love weather.

To: Tim and Jo; Jon and Chinatsu; Beth
Subject: Special again
An Island of Mists and Changes

'So what's the weather like?' people ask. ' Endless days of hot tropical sun shining out of a clear blue sky, I expect.'

Well, not exactly. In fact hardly right at all! Technically St Helena is within the tropics and the sun is often hot when it shines out of clear blue skies but that is definitely not all the time. Napoleon's view of gloomy days with mist, damp, mouldy clothes and dripping walls, might be closer to the mark for at least half the year. To start with, to say just 'mist' is far too simple as it has many forms and many moods. Some mornings one wakes up to an eerie, dull light and the drip, drip, drip of water on the banana leaves. A glance out of the window shows nothing but a still soup of mist and the shadowy forms of nearby buildings and trees. Flagstaff Hill and The Barn are completely blotted out. In winter this can go on all day, yet often at other times, within an hour or two the mist will have disappeared leaving everything bright and clear.

On other days when out and about you can see a great mass of mist rolling in from the sea, increasing in speed, unstoppable as it moves along the valleys, up the slopes enveloping all before it. Cliffs, woods, houses, fields are swallowed up. The mist, now like an amorphous and insatiable creature, climbing, and consuming forests and farms, peaks and ridges and then tumbling and billowing down the other side eventually to dissipate, energy spent, succumbing to the warmth of the sun. Again, sometimes the mist can be seen hanging like so many strands of candyfloss strung over the dark forests of the steep valley sides; or as a vast woolly cap perching on Flagstaff and The Barn!

From mist to rain. There is often a fine intermittent drizzle, which is usually totally disregarded by everyone. It doesn't wet one very much and it doesn't last very long. There is also the heavy rain which comes at night and can last for some time though that frequently arrives in waves like an aerial version of the sea. Then there is the steady drenching rain. One night we were actually woken by a sudden thunderous clatter as the rain fell in heavy drops on the metal roof, threatening to come right through. Perhaps it is so loud because the clouds are caught by the island as they race across the ocean and the raindrops are huge and don't have far to fall. I drove back from choir practice one evening through really torrential rain just like the real tropics. Too many days of this means that the steep slopes of the valleys become unstable and rock-falls on to roads, houses and gardens are the order of the day.

Lest this sounds too depressing there are many days when the sun shines out of a thinly cloudy sky and times when hot sun and blue skies are truly tropical. After the rain the air is so clean and clear that all the colours in the landscape are sharp and bright. As I drive to school looking at Diana's Peak, the brilliant green against the clear blue sky, it seems as if I could reach out of the window and touch the summit.

The air is very rarely entirely still, as might be expected of an island in the path of the trades as they blow across the Atlantic. Often it is a gentle breeze, sometimes a strong wind oblivious to those battling around the exposed golf course, and occasionally a good heavy blow. Some amazingly sculpted trees bear witness to the prevailing wind; a young, spindly trunk crowned with an extravagant Elvis quiff; or a clump of mature trees huddled on an exposed slope like a bunch of old, grey men, bent as one, turning their backs and finally yielding to the endless pressure of the wind.

Seasons are distinguished by slightly more or less rain, more or less dripping mist and temperatures that are cold enough for shoes, a jumper and a fleece or hot enough for sleeveless tops, flip-flops and swimming. But yet again it depends where you are - down in stifling Jamestown, out at windy Sandy Bay, here in misty Longwood or in cold St Paul's (which is where they put the Governor's residence it being considered the most healthy location).

Saints will always point out that there is a constant change over time and place. At church in St Paul's District four miles away one is asked 'what like is the weather in Longwood?' When dressing for town one must be clothed in layers to be removed as necessary on the descent, or at least at the end of it! Plans for school children to have sports practice on the secondary school playing field on Francis Plain are not cancelled because it is raining at the Middle School in St Pauls. A trip on a fishing boat to see the dolphins is not postponed because the sky is grey and the wind is blowing; it will all have changed in a couple of hours. And the sun does shine. When sports day came there was a brief shower as everyone set off and then the sun shone bright and strong throughout the day – no shade, no relief. I needed factor 30 and my golfing umbrella to survive.

As in Africa the skies here seem so immense especially when filled with clouds. On many days complicated patterns form with deeper and deeper layers as strange and distant lands are created in the towering cumulus as if in a different time and dimension. There are glorious sunsets of gold, pink, peach or fiery red.

So far there has been just one truly memorable storm. I was standing in the graveyard above the church one night waiting for people to come for choir practice. The air was full of a great noise in the woods on the slope across the lane as the wind fought its way through the treetops. On the ground around me the changing light patterns across the graves and grass looked for all the world like an old black and white movie, and up in the sky there was the moon dashing through the scudding clouds racing across the sky. Fantastic!

The wind and the rain continued all night and in the morning there was no power. More importantly there was no tea - until the camping gaz was hauled out of the cupboard and the day could be faced with equanimity.

Date: 24th May
To: Beth
Subject: St Helena Day

We had Wednesday off this week, so after a leisurely start dad and I went across to the school to check on the start of the AS level maths exam then made our way down into town. There had been a service and speeches by the Governor and others in the main square, which we felt we could miss. There were stalls and competitions and things much resembling a village fete. The weather was very pleasant and the atmosphere quite jolly with everyone greeting each other and chatting earnestly as if they hadn't seen each other for months rather than the day before.

It is good to see that people of all ages come along to this sort of event but then there is not much else going on! We dutifully had a go at everything and then, at around 3pm, I went to the museum which was celebrating its first birthday in its new home. The building (just back from the waterfront), used to be the old powerhouse but there was a great effort by the Saints to get the place more or less reconstructed and now it is an extremely attractive edifice with an excellent display. It is certainly an asset to the island and visitors love it. I found myself in charge of the shop area. I sold a good number of T-shirts, books, badges and postcards and am seriously considering a change in my career - no hassle and no homework and best of all no kids!! Or if kids do come I can send them away if they don't behave! There is also no money but considering what I am paid I doubt whether I'd notice.

I also went tadpole hunting for science this week. I found the pool/large puddle under the hedge on the edge of our housing compound last week, when I hit a brilliant ball that was supposed to go on the 9th green! Well you can't expect a good stroke, distance and direction all at the same time - I'm not Tiger Woods after all.

Date: 1st June
To: Rosemary
Subject: Broadcasting career

I am gradually losing that thrill and earnestness about teaching that I used to have. Well at least for teaching children. I'd absolutely love to do some more training of adult teachers as I did in The Gambia, but I'm not too sure that I'll get the opportunity - we shall have to wait and see.

However I have at last done something that I have always wanted to do and that is to get involved with radio. Richard and I have done the first of a series of programmes for Radio St Helena. There is a programme called 'Classical Mix'. You put together an hour of your favourite pieces of classical music with comments and so on and then go armed with your box of CDs to the radio station (a large hut next to my school) and record it ready for Sunday evening. Our first one goes out tonight (with a repeat on Wednesday) and we will be taking our turn once a month. I think it is a sop for those who do not want wall-to-wall country and western, which is the main fare on radio for this island. Rather fun and something a bit different for us! We might not sound very chatty as, being conscious that others are listening, I at least put on that special 'clear voice' for the occasion - one can't immediately overcome 30 years of being a teacher.

I guess I shall have to face tonight's marking eventually and will finish this e-mail only commenting that I have not before seen clergy blowing a kiss to the altos at the 'peace'.

Leave is not far away now.

Date: 15th June
To: Jon and Chinatsu
Subject: Queen's Birthday Party

Yet another four-day week, great. I think I shall suggest that this is the way of the future. It is not as if it will make much difference to the children. You can tell that I am heading for SATS and the kids are pretty grim at the moment.

So - our entertainment this weekend was THE garden party for the Queen's Birthday. Garden is not quite accurate as a marquee was put up on the tarmac car park in front of Plantation House as it was thought that the grass would be too wet. People actually wore hats! I didn't have one. But I had water in my ear from the hurried shower and was dehydrated from slipping in a quick game of golf before the jollifications so my head went all echoey and I couldn't hear properly. I was making what I hoped were appropriate answers and was terrified of keeling over as everyone would have said I was drunk - on one G&T - how mortifying. I was really quite glad when the bishop swept out in his flowing purple robes saying to me as he went, 'such a shame being bishop and having to be the first one to leave so that everyone else is then also able to go.' Yes, such is the protocol here. Not quite sure what century we are in sometimes.

Hope you are managing to keep up with Dan as he races round the house, Chinatsu.

Date: 28th June
To: Beth
Subject: Dawn and Sandwiches

Most impressive – you were up all night doing Red Cross duty at the Goldney Ball and saw in the dawn – well done.

Don't think I have done 'dawn' for an awful long time. Nothing is exciting enough or goes on long enough on this island to last to dawn and apart from fishermen and nurses, dawn is a definite no-no on this island. You don't actually need a dawn start to begin a safari to the other end of the island or even to drive round it a few times should you be desperate enough to want to do so.

Actually that is quite unfair as I think many women get up very early to do the household chores and make the absolute mountain of sandwiches required to enable the menfolk and children to survive through the day! Believe me I am not joking. The workmen on the house below us arrive at 7ish and settle down to sandwiches and tea. Work for possibly a couple of hours and then break for sandwiches and tea. Then of course there is the major stop for lunch - possibly sandwiches or a box of spare ribs or sausages or a rice mix. Finally they have to stop at 3:30pm so that they have enough time to eat their last sandwiches before getting the minibus home at 4:00pm to another part of the island in time for a proper meal. The kids at school are much the same!

I have been enjoying myself recently by taking up sketching again. I have been trying to capture some of the views from the golf course and have drawn some of the flowers we have here - morning-glory, hibiscus, arum lilies, agapanthus, and even bougainvillea. Do these bring back memories? There again I recall that botany is not really your thing and 'big blue ones', 'red trumpet ones' or those 'pretty yellow' flowers is about the extent of your powers of recognition in that field.

Date: 28th June
To: Beth
Subject: Surprise visit

Well fancy that then - assuming all goes well, and things are looking very hopeful - we shall actually be seeing you here in three weeks' time. What a nice surprise, your dad really does come up trumps at times.

Now clothes - this is our winter of course. We have actually had it very fine and dry for about 3 weeks and everyone is commenting about it and reminding each other that last year it rained for some time on every day or night for 3 months.

- Basically it is a bit like Africa in that you need layers.
- You need some warm stuff like a fleece for going up the peak and a couple of thin jumpers.
- As for the rest, all sorts of tops that go with trousers - mix of sleeveless and others as I don't think you will feel the cool like us.
- I know I said that they are old fashioned in some ways here but you don't have to worry about having to wear skirts and everything stretching below the knees like Malawi - shorts and trousers are fine.
- One of your long wrap round skirts would cover the problem of an invitation to somewhere smarter, though we haven't had many of those.
- If you come and help out at school it gets perishing cold up there at times.
- Trainers would be very useful, all the children and half the adults wear them.
- Also walking boots but Dad has mentioned those.

Now I mentioned school. We will of course be working for some of the time you are here as unfortunately they go on into August, however I think that it is highly likely that my school could well be interested if you would like to help out LSA style.

This will give you something to think about while you are marching along Hadrian's Wall. It is something we haven't done yet but would like to. I hope you both enjoy it.

To: Tim and Jo; Jon and Chinatsu; Beth
Subject: A special as promised

Instructions for driving to school.

First back the car out of the doorless garage, the buckled door has been propped up against the wall since before we arrived.
Drive out of the dilapidated holiday-camp-looking compound and over a cattle grid (to stop the donkeys wandering in).
Wave to the three–day worker just coming in to do his stint. These people are the unemployed who are required to do three days a week on some sort of organised directed community work in order to get their benefit.
Drive at 15mph past the golf club, the infant school and Napoleon's house and along the main road of Longwood.
Wave to the two teaching assistants on their way to school.
Wave to the old chap who is staggering across the Green looking as if he is still part of the drinking session from the previous night. This convivial activity seems to happen nearly every evening outside the little supermarket.
Drive up to the gates of the village and turn left away from Deadwood Plain, the site of the Boer prisoner of war camp.
Begin journey along winding narrow road on constant look out for traffic coming the other way.

Wave to the group of ladies waiting for their regular lift in a truck. I haven't yet found out where they go. Meet minibus on the bend and wait in a wider piece of road.
Wave to the driver.
Drive in second gear, at sedate 20mph along road with a view across a valley to very steep slopes scattered with scrub. Round bend to view a beautiful valley heavily wooded.
Wave to lady with small boy waiting for transport.
Hutts Gate junction has a small shop, a bar (another venue for regular evening conviviality) and St Matthew's church – wave to people waiting for their lift. Third gear now- goody! then pull in sharply as a car appears round the corner.
Wave to the driver.
Now prepare to negotiate the first of six hairpin bends on the journey to school.
Change into first gear, peep horn and start round and up the first bend, nothing coming this time but at the top is another tight and narrow bend and there is a landrover. Creep past carefully. Wave to the driver, then on in heightened anticipation – this is the bit where I might just have a chance to get up into fourth gear and go 40mph for all of 300 yards – the exhilaration! Made my day – now down quickly into second as I approach the bridge and bend at the end of the valley.

Continue along side of the valley on narrow road with prolific flax plants lining the upper side and providing perches for the brilliant scarlet cardinals. The other birds I see all the time are the mynah birds with their yellow eyes, striking patterns of white, black and brown and their strutting posture. There is a group of them that congregates on our roof every morning and has a real gossip before beginning the business of the day. Round yet another bend and check across the valley, spot a vehicle coming my way.

Where will we meet? If it is this side then I have to stop as I am on the way down, if I get round the end of the valley and start the climb then he has to wait in a passing place for me. People are very good about this on the whole. The problem is there is often no view. Either way we wave.

On in a mixture of second and occasionally third and I take my eyes briefly off the road to see a farmer with cattle on the steep slopes where ridges of pasture ripple down like the furrows on a bloodhound's brow. Whooooa …. Confronted by an intimidating lorry. I decide to scuttle into a sort of passing place despite being on the way up.

Wave.

Concentrate at least until I get to my favourite valley. Some three-day workers are clearing the vegetation overhanging the road near the turning to Sandy Bay, which is on the other side of the island – about three miles away – and a place for an even more exciting drive. It was at this junction that there were masses of wild arum lilies growing on the side of the road when I first came.

Dead rat on the road.

Now on to my favourite part. As I come round the headland there is a view of a heavily wooded valley and the tops of a couple of houses. There are usually pairs of white fairy terns which fly close together weaving patterns against the backdrop of the dark green foliage of the forest trees below. But no time to enjoy it as now we have the three hairpin bends down into the valley and the turning to Prince Andrew's Secondary School. Because of the school this is a fairly hazardous part of the route as the mini buses that collect the children from all over the island hurtle round the bends with hands on the horn in their efforts to get school children, teachers, assistants, admin staff and sundry others to their right destinations by 9.0 clock. They don't always wave! Another dead rat! The council must have put down rat poison again.

Climbing cautiously up the final hillside I pass the Boer cemetery with its ranks of severe white graves standing as a reminder of the typhoid epidemic amongst the prisoners. The gates at the end of the drive to Plantation House (the Governor's Residence) face me at the junction with the road down to town. Turn inland, wave to random person standing in the lych-gate of the cathedral. Finally change into first gear and turn up the drive leading to the wireless station and my school with the commanding view of the High Knoll Fort guarding the town, Flagstaff Hill and my village, and 180° of ocean!

If it is a Friday just before 4:00 I go and collect Dad from school. We then join the road near Plantation House and set off to Half Tree Hollow and the descent into town. Half Tree Hollow (don't you love the name) is a really scary place as there has been a great deal of building of one storey homes on this slope which is bare of vegetation and feels as if it is at a 30° angle. It ends in 400ft cliffs and a drop to the ocean. The trouble when you are driving down the very open slope is that you feel if your brakes failed you would just carry straight off the cliff and out over the sea and then realise that playing 'road runner' was not much fun!

Having made it down to the old fortifications at the top of Ladder Hill I have the choice of abandoning the car and going down the 700 steps straight into town or holding my breath and setting off on the notorious Ladder Hill road. I tuck myself into a little passing place and cautiously squint down the narrow road to see if it is clear enough for me to pluck up courage and start on down. Once started there is no going back. It is a bit like playing cowboys and Indians in the woods. I look for the next hiding place and gauge whether I can get there before I am faced with the up coming traffic. The fact that it is only single track, there is a steep descent with many twists and turns and that there is a solid rock face on one side and a sheer drop the other side of a two foot wall, just adds to the fun. Let's not forget that I am still expected to take my hand off the wheel to wave to everyone I pass. I usually make sure that I do not do it at 5 past 4 on a Friday afternoon when the whole of town seems to be coming the other way.

Once down in the town I make my way along the one main street and through the arch in the wall to the waterfront. Turn right for the swimming pool and left for Donny's meeting and eating place. We usually visit them in that order and fortify ourselves sufficiently to take the journey up the other side of the valley and home. Actually this is generally rather easier but we do it in the dark. So now you have a picture of the driving. Those who have never left the island have never seen a traffic light or a roundabout and have never travelled more than 40 miles an hour. ……

Date: 12th July
To: Beth
Subject: A hint!

Good, glad to know all the plans and tickets are sorted. Be prepared for questions about how we're enjoying ourselves as soon as any casual acquaintance knows who you are. We are thoroughly enjoying ourselves and everything is fine.

Date: 10th July
To: Rosemary
Subject: Volcanoes and food parcels

Lovely to hear from you again, thank you for your e-mail from Scotland. I wonder if you actually had a rest there. We have just been watching the most amazing programme on volcanoes. I just love them - such incredible and terrifying power, wonderful billowing patterns of gas and steam, that marvellous and unstoppable flow of molten lava, overwhelming statistics - as the Americans say – awesome. Then one thinks of puny, petty mankind. However I suppose on reflection perhaps, just sometimes, humans can also show the most amazing power - that of love - not showy and spectacular but of incredible strength, unstoppable and seemingly inexhaustable. It gives one pause...

But to get back to one tiny volcanic pimple - if we don't get a food parcel soon we shall not need a dieting regime to achieve the 'appropriate weight for our height'. At present there are no potatoes, no onions, no veg or fruit (even bananas are in short supply), no eggs and very little milk. I was reduced to pulling up sustenance from the lawn this weekend. Well perhaps we are not starving yet but we are definitely waiting on the ship coming back from Cape Town sometime soon and without the engine breaking down again.

Paradoxically we had a taste of our first yoghurts since before Christmas just this last week - bliss. All the problems are due to the fact that the ship went off to UK on its month long trip so we needed to make do here with what we had, and stores had run rather low. Definitely useful to be a local and in the exchange set up. When the ship came back from UK it had odd things like some dried goods and special dairy products like long-life yoghurts but none of the fresh stuff. Some of that did come on the next trip from Cape Town but most of it was snapped up so quickly that I never got a look in, so we are waiting for the next visit already. There is only so much tuna, pork and rice one can take. I meant it about pulling up stuff from the lawn. I noticed some parsley growing in the grass outside the back door by the path to the car.

Beth tells us she had a great time at the church fete and everyone makes her feel so much that she belongs. It means a great deal to her and to us especially in this situation. The fete sounded an excellent occasion as usual and I really did miss being there. The latest fund raising thing here was a Casino Night at the Governor's residence. The ship was in and the purser brought all the equipment – blackjack and roulette tables and so on - which was then set up in Plantation House. Nearly a hundred people (expats and islanders) arrived dressed up in their black tie and glad rags, and for the entrance fee of £5 for 25 chips it was off to the tables. Some of the young Saint girls from the island and the ship's crew had been trained as croupiers though the maths presented a challenge at times. The aim was to see who managed to win the greatest number of chips by the end of the evening and the prize was a trip on the RMS St Helena.

It was one of the few opportunities when I could dress up in my peacock-blue sari with its elaborate gold embroidery. I felt elegant just putting it on. There was an excellent atmosphere with plenty of chat and good humour and reasonable consumption of alcohol. There were a whole lot of Saints there that I don't think I had ever seen before. Over £600 was raised for the hospital, which apparently is very impressive for this island.

Beth probably told you that she is coming out to see us in just over a fortnight. A bit of a cry for help and a last minute rush but it is now fixed and we are really looking forward to it as you can imagine.

Look after yourself.

Date: 15th July
To: Beth
Subject: Bon Voyage

Your special holiday starts when you leave Jon's in Cove: day and night in up-market Cotswolds hideaway; exclusive air transport (as used by royalty); top of the (available) hotels on remote tropical island; luxury cruise; long holiday close to the former holiday home of an emperor. Finally another cruise! (Which reminds me of the story of my parents visiting Applecross, on a peninsular opposite Skye. I think it's one of the highest public roads in the UK to get there, and they were driving it at dusk with mist all around. My father said to mother, while waiting at hotel reception, that he was never going to drive that road again, they would return round the coast. The receptionist quietly pointed out that he *would be driving it again*, as it was the only way out.)

So I hope you enjoy the first cruise. Enjoy yourself. Looking forward to your arrival. Lots of love, Dad

Date: 3rd August
To: Jon and Chinatsu
Subject: New Job!

Dear SIR and Chinatsu

What excellent news from you on Friday, thank you for the call and many congratulations. What exactly is your job title going to be, I didn't quite take it in? It is nice to get things settled so that you can plan a little way into the future and not have to preface everything by 'if'. I gather that Chinatsu's family were pleased as well as it is such a well-known Japanese firm.

Things have been pretty hectic here since Beth arrived as you can imagine. It being towards the end of term there seem to be so many things to do and I don't really know where the time goes, but no doubt we will get most things done. It is really funny in some ways because ever since Beth has been here we have had all sorts of things in the shops because we had two ship visits in a very short time. This has meant that the shelves are full and there is a fair amount of choice. This gives a totally false picture of the normal state of things but I don't know if she believes us!

We have managed to provide a variety of experiences including a trip to Donny's of course and a combined schools' music concert which she has put on video, plus an inter schools' football and rounders tournament. You can't say that we haven't tried to show her what she is in for if she goes for teaching. We have also been up Diana's Peak and I have taken her out on the golf course several times. However this was not a good idea since she has picked it up immediately and is belting the ball way down the fairway.

Date: 10th August
To: Tim and Jo
Subject: Where are you?

Not entirely sure where you are now. When do you go on leave? It seems that it will be hotter for you in UK than it is for you in Rwanda. It is certainly hotter than here at the moment though we have done very well since Beth came. This is supposed to be winter and the wettest and coldest time of the year. They call it 'scruffy August' but until a day or so ago we had had no rain for nearly 6 weeks and the temperatures have been fine. Things are changing now but we managed to have a great day yesterday. We had arranged with a friend to go out on a whale-hunting trip as there are humped back whales around the island at the moment and although we did not see the whales we did have a good time. There were about 16 of us and we went out in a reasonably fast moving motorboat. The weather was very kind despite beginning to change and we saw the 2-300 dolphins. Beth was very impressed despite her experience on that scuba diving trip in Indonesia. We went further along the coast of the island and did some bird spotting and then on the way home stopped off at Lemon Valley for some of the party including Beth and dad to have a swim.

After a late lunch at Donny's we visited Sandy Bay (I think I sent you a photo from there) and returned home for some relaxation before going for a lovely anniversary meal at Farm Lodge, the only really smart place to eat on the island. Someone else to do the cooking and really lovely food in a very homely but unobtrusive atmosphere.

LAST WEEK of term - much relief filled with considerable sympathy for the other teachers as they will all have to be back again after just a 2 week holiday - for the beginning of a new school year!! Whereas we, of course, will be coming on LEAVE. At the moment I feel much as I enjoy living here and the people I live and work with, I need to get away to see family and join the rest of the world – just to check it is really there. I would never have believed I would be saying this but a visit to a normal supermarket and a bit of clothes shopping in a big store actually sounds quite attractive.

58

PART TWO
Date: 7th September
To: Beth
Subject: Return to exile

We arrived back in St Helena at last to be greeted by mist and rain. Exile is so inviting!

The flight to Cape Town was very good considering the length of it and Business Class does make a great difference. After a shower we hit the shops in Cape Town's wonderful new Waterfront. Well we didn't really but we did achieve a little essential shopping of the liquid variety and one or two bits of clothing for me (including a rather expensive silk kaftan) but we didn't succeed with the golf clubs.

There were some 'interesting' fellow passengers on the ship. We met up with Paddy and John who were on the boat down, then there was the bishop. I still disagree with him on many things but he, as always, was a great raconteur and a group of us had a hilarious final evening.

We also had a group of three MPs (part of a Commonwealth Parliamentary Committee) and they haven't exactly improved the opinion held of that breed, by all those travelling with them on the ship. One in particular was rude, arrogant and lazy. He did not appear to get into conversation with anyone (especially Saints) other than those in his party, except to give the odd expat such as me the third degree. He did this whilst we were lying out on the sun deck. He kept blasting questions at me, not really listening to the answers, especially when I suggested that he might like to talk to the various experts we happened to be carrying on board. I know somewhat less than the power station expert about why the wind generators were not working and considerably less than Dougie about the present state of the social services. As to what the Governor did all day (he was not on board) and whether the island was run efficiently or not - I'd had enough so I said, "I have spent many years working abroad, particularly in African countries, and I have learnt to look and to listen and to make no public comment." That seemed to shut him up a bit.

He had obviously read nothing and apparently when he first heard he was coming he thought it was in the Caribbean and when he found it wasn't, initially refused to come. (This was all in the local newspaper in his constituency and picked up by the St Helena Herald.) However I must say that the others were better. There was also an FCO man who was really lovely and very impressive. He looked and listened and chatted to just about everyone and even came down to the Crew Disco in the bowels of the ship to have his head pounded by extremely loud rock music in a very confined space - he lasted longer than we did down there.

We did the usual games and dad won the shuffle-board. I actually swam one day - for about 2 minutes! We also had a BBQ on the sun deck on the last night which was rather fun.

The first evening on the island was spent in a two-hour service with ALL the trimmings (robes, candles, bells - including that telephone thing - and incense) as the bishop was ordaining Brother Chris. There were about 20 people from the ship, which was nice, various expats and a reasonable number of Saints so the cathedral was fairly full. We had the choir up from St James and all choir members sang an anthem but the choirs hadn't practised together and certainly not with the organ. Dad and I were sight-reading though it wasn't exactly difficult and the organist still insisted on singing while playing - nothing new there then! Oh yes and someone had taken all the service books from our side so it was one between three.

I must have been refreshed by leave as I landed in another two-hour service the next evening. Brother - now Father - Chris was taking his first communion service which happened to be at Hutts Gate in that little church up on the exposed hill towards Longwood. The wind was howling round the building and in through the nooks and crannies and the rain was pounding on the corrugated roof as the bishop (for once in a minor role) and Father Chris swirled around in a sea of red robes, candles and incense. The resident choir of church ladies sang and chanted at a somewhat slower pace than the organist and the visiting choir members, however we gradually adjusted ourselves. A memorable service and the bishop gave a good sermon. Dad was at a parents' meeting at the secondary school.

UK suddenly seems a long way away and a lovely warm memory. It is now back to driving at 20 miles an hour, cooking tuna in twenty different ways and waiting until the ship unloads the long awaited crates of onions! Would you believe we came back with enough strepsils to fill a chemist shop only to find the shelves groaning with them. Mind you there is no decent powder and soap so we are using the stuff you left. The bed was horribly damp and almost sticky to touch so we are very glad to have the electric blanket.

Date: 15th October
To: Beth
Subject: We saw whales.

I can't believe how I managed to leave this off the first e-mail. Yes we saw a whale - in fact we saw two. We were somewhere between the Cape and here but nearer the Cape (very precise), sitting in the sun-lounge having lunch, when the captain announces over the tannoy that if anyone was interested there were whales on the port bow. Immediate abandonment of lunch and a seemly rush outside (after all many of us were British) - and there on the port bow were two hump-back whales. Their dorsal fins and backs kept appearing only to sink down again. However as we drew level with them and just a couple of hundred yards away one of them breached - its great black and white body came almost all out of the water. It turned and thumped back into the sea with a big splash, but not before we got a good look at all the barnacles and stuff growing on it. Fantastic, then as if that wasn't enough, it did it again. Whew. Then they swam away and the ocean was empty once more. I kept going over it for days afterwards.

Date: 16th October
To: Beth
Subject: All change

Don't know why I keep forgetting to tell you stuff. The other bit of immediate news is that we are going to have Viv's house - the one at the front of the compound with more privacy and a fantastic view. We will be moving in the middle of November.

You have got round to getting insurance over your tickets to Rwanda haven't you? (yes mum stop fussing/nagging/worrying) and of course you have insured your 'cello for the new academic year.

Date: 19th October
To: Tim and Jo
Subject: Home-sickness

Nothing much has happened since our last e-mail in fact nothing much seems to happen on this island at all except gossip about who is now the partner of whom and who has gone off the island or just returned. Of course we are now in the long break whilst the ship goes to UK and before any of the cruise ships come. It is generally quite cold and very damp and misty at the moment. I remember when I arrived at this time last year thinking to myself, 'what have I come to?' Now I know and I can't say that I am that excited, except about the scenery. Still no doubt I will cheer up when the home-sickness wears off.

I got back to doing some drawing today - relaxing after the combined Harvest Festival and Baptism service this morning (quite appropriate if you look at it one way - sowing seed and growing things). What news of all your exams Jo?

Date: 21st October
To: All
Subject: Who's who?

I think I ought to fill you in on a few of the people of the island as I have now got to know quite a number of them, though for the most part the relationships are kept fairly superficial. I suppose this is only reasonable as expats come and go all the time. Locals know you are only there for a short time and it is not especially likely that you will meet again. Of course we have met this situation before haven't we, and apart from a few notable exceptions this has indeed been the case.

A SPECIAL
Island ladies

The men may think that they are in charge but the island is really run by the women.

Here are a few of the ones that I meet regularly. There are a number of others in the heart of the island's main institutions and committees but I don't meet many of them often, although we all know who they are and I inevitably hear quite a bit about them.

Edith
Bright, cheerful, energetic, in her seventies somewhere (I think). Into and part of everything – she must be or has been on every committee going; works tirelessly for the museum; is very welcoming to expats – she likes to think 'outside the box' and get other peoples' views on things; loves entertaining; she is a strong supporter of the church and has a great love of golf and so has to juggle the two very carefully. She has travelled all over the world including on the Trans Siberian Railway. A lady with a definite mind of her own.

Lydia
Nearly ninety; rather thin with the worn and weather-beaten face of one who has lived a hard life, and much of that out of doors; lives on her own in a house attached to the golf clubhouse; son keeps an eye on her; has other family overseas; brought up grandchild from a baby (common occurrence on the island); keeps chickens; always seen at any Longwood function; loves to chat and always ready to talk about her years in UK when she went to work in Yorkshire under very tough conditions; does well exchanging her precious eggs for variety of other produce.

Joy
Eldest of ten children (large families used to be very common on the island); siblings show due respect even if tinged with frustration; thin face surrounded by lovely thick, shoulder-length grey hair; always looks worried or anxious; deputy head of the secondary school; choir mistress; belongs to everything especially to do with the church and education; sometimes a bit disorganised and definitely overworked and as a result nearly always late; very concerned for the life of the church; interested in and friendly to expats possibly somewhat tougher with Saints; very patient with children.

Cathy
Expat came as VSO over thirty years ago; married to a Saint (there are a number of 'mixed' marriages on the island); tall,

angular with short, salt and pepper hair; often in floral print dress and flat sandals; musical; used to teach; good earnest Christian; somewhat acerbic manner; efficient; island councillor but exasperated by ponderous and conservative committee system of running most things on the island; has very firm views.

Pat Henry

Necessary to give full name as there are so few names that many are duplicated (especially with the men – we have a tea towel with the family names of the island). Late middle age; friendly, bright eyes, round face, giggles and laughs and enjoys a joke; strong Sandy Bay accent; good with craft work including knitting; excellent with children – firm and effective; has standards; works very hard as teaching assistant; married to Cedric who works on the wharf and on their own land; unlike some on the island always ready to learn new things (with a bit of encouragement) eg computer; slow to criticise; difficult to detect her thinking – have to look for signs.

Carolyn

In her thirties; two children; husband works for Cable and Wireless; extremely bright family; trained as a teacher; family went to Malta for two years then returned; more modern and wider view on life; still supports main island traditions; good rapport with children; wants things to move forward on the island; if her own children not stretched enough says she will go abroad again; prepared to make a stand.

Leslie

Middle aged, cheerful; has what looks like a limp from polio but I haven't asked her; always ready for a chat; does housework and ironing for me and several others on the compound; very concerned for everybody; has some ducks, and some land which she works with her son; has an encyclopaedic memory of past residents of the compound;

always seems to know ahead of time when something is going to run short.

Men

I was thinking about the men but I know much less about them, there are only a few in primary schools and I only see most of the island men's very public persona. They do like to take up public positions and be on Government committees but there seem to be rather fewer of them on the committees that actually get things done! I would be had for libel if I wrote some of the things on the gossip channel!

Date: 25th October
To: Beth
Subject: Tips from experience

The PGCE course sounds as if it is going very well indeed. I think it was all so much more muddled up in our day. I don't know why you are worrying about 'dance'. I don't think that I would have the first idea how to go about teaching it and I can do it. One way or another I have managed to avoid it for my whole teaching career.

Having 30 kids doing gym in the UK scared the pants off me so I off-loaded it after one lesson! Swapped with another member of staff so I did his RE - marginally less dangerous. Tell Ed he just has to pick the kid who can do a forward roll to give a demonstration (believe me there is always one), not give an Oscar performance himself - he might be had up for assault as all the kids fall about with cracked ribs from laughing. But perhaps he has worked that one out for himself.

I have generally had a good half term though Dad and I did a radio programme mid week. All was well until the last 10 mins when everything went pear shaped. Still the good news is that we have the December 21st slot for our next one so we will be able to have a great time with all sorts of proper Christmas music.

By the way I think that Tim is in UK soon, possibly next weekend to do his assessment for his next grade. Do send some encouraging words you know how he so hates those role-play things and gets incredibly nervous. I think it is quite important for his prospects that he passes it.

Date: 9th November
To: Jon and Chinatsu
Subject: Food again and Remembrance on the waterfront

I think I have made a tactical mistake – as you know how much I hate cooking and what have I done but invited a domestic science teacher (well that's what they used to be called) and a South African food fanatic for supper. This is for a date two days *before* the ship returns after its six-week break away. There is already a worse than usual shortage of fresh fruit and vegetables due to the drought. Hey-ho - as long as there is some sort of food on the table at least the husbands won't mind.

How come all my thoughts seem to revolve around food? Luckily I was out to a farewell supper on Friday and the Golf Club Centenary dinner dance last night so that's two meals I didn't have to cook. We actually did lots of two-step and quickstep type dancing at which the Saints are very good, so that was rather fun. This was a jolly occasion with the golfing fraternity out in full force and very few expats to be seen, though the 'blood man' (pathologist at the hospital), the Governor and one or two others do play. The men do the BBQ of course and the women the mountains of rice and lots of salads (the Saints rarely seem at a loss for these commodities).

It seems that you two have been dancing attendance on your older brother just recently, Jon. He did appreciate it by the way, and it obviously paid off as he passed that wretched exam - what a relief.

We had our Remembrance Service down on the waterfront today. All the uniformed groups turned out in full force and the island managed to muster three bands! The island's councillors were there as was the bishop in full purple regalia along with the Governor and his ostrich feathers (actually this is the last outing for them as they are being phased out - the feathers I mean). Richard and I decided to go incognito, as it were, not in choir robes with the massed church choirs. The service was very moving in places especially as we sang the hymn 'Oh God our help in ages past' with the sound of the waves crashing on the shore a few metres away. A wreath was thrown on the water from a boat, over the wreck of a ship that was sunk in the bay in the war, with all hands lost but two. Part of the superstructure appears at low tide and the whole shape can be seen shimmering rather eerily through the clear waters from the top of Ladder Hill.

There are three ships' visits later this month and into December. This means farewell events for people leaving, then there is all the planning for forthcoming Christmas activities. So, it is feeling a little more lively on the island at the moment. However I said to dad that this is definitely the last Christmas I am having away from everyone.

Right, now back to 'parts of a flower' and 'testing the strength of three different kinds of cotton', with 'pollution of rivers' with Year Six as a bonus.

Date: 23rd November
To: Beth
Subject: Moving and Reproduction

Whew - what a week! I guess I keep forgetting until too late - despite having done it over 30 times - what it means to move house even if it is just down the road. We moved on Thursday and we are just about feeling sort of normal now on Sunday afternoon. I took Thursday off so I have to pay back the day in the holidays. We were supposed to have help from the Public Works Dept (PWD) but somehow that didn't seem to be happening so in the end dad and I moved almost everything, assisted by Mary and Ricky who also live on Piccolo. During the morning someone turned up to switch the cookers and wire them in and then the plumbers came to do the washing machine ie fix one hose onto the end of a pipe.

Finally a couple of chaps came at 2:00pm to help us move. At least we had left the freezer and the filing cabinet for them. One advantage of this particular move was that I didn't have to make any decisions - firstly we were moving everything and all to the same place and secondly in general, since the houses are exactly the same in design, I didn't have to decide where everything had to go. We now have a fair amount of privacy, our own garden area and that superb view of Flagstaff and The Barn and the sea, with absolutely no houses at all (well there is the Met Station in the distance but that doesn't count).

I went into work on Friday to be faced with teaching Human Reproduction to the Year 6. 'Now we start with the naming of parts so here they are all clearly labelled on an OHP transparency.' Some of the girls covered their faces and looked aghast but after the initial shock all of them were, of course, seriously interested and asked some good sensible questions. They also told me, totally uninvited, more than I needed to know about what some of their parents said and did. At one point I had to sneak to the back of the class when they were drawing the relevant diagram to check up in a dictionary what a dildo was! (OK so you have a poor innocent mum – did they have them in Africa?) It was what I thought but luckily by then the talk had moved on. There were also some questions on condoms, not surprisingly, and I answered those that needed a scientific answer but steered well clear of why some were banana or strawberry flavoured!

Saturday we had the first solid day of rain for about six months so it was very welcome but not quite what we wanted when trying to sort the house out. The ship came and went and is now on its way to Cape Town. We didn't even see it. Now I have lessons to prepare including part two with Year 6 – 'the Life Cycle of a human being' so presumably we are in for another round of questions.

Date: 30th November
To: Beth
Subject: Condoms, Concerts and Weddings

What a weekend. It started with that really super e-mail from you. I am delighted to hear that the schoolwork is going well and you have had fun on teaching practice. I do feel that I have to sort out an apparent misunderstanding - I was not actually teaching the year 6 about dildos or the relative merits of the different flavours of condoms - just in case you find yourself in an absorbing discussion on the contents of the QCA document for KS2 science and start quoting me.

Which reminds me, when I was telling the staff at break about the condom enquiries and everyone was laughing and chatting, one teacher pondered for a minute and then asked (quite genuinely it seemed) 'why are condoms flavoured as a matter of fact?' Silence for a moment and then someone said ' I don't think I know, we'll have to ask Mrs Fisher- well Mrs Fisher?' After I worked out they really were asking and had all eyes on me - I thought quickly and decided they weren't ready for the explicit answer or at least I wasn't going to give it, so replied 'well let's say they are put in places you might not expect them to be put!' - a slight pause and then they all started laughing, the bell went and they all went off wondering if the vision they were conjuring up really was the answer!

At lunchtime the Year 6 teacher comes into the staff room and says - 'Carl tells me that you said that he was ready to make babies.' - OK, so what I actually said was that at 11 years some boys could! How come there wasn't all this excitement when we were doing birds, bees and flowers?

Now for other news. Friday night dad and I went over to Levelwood for a local fund raising concert. We took Mary (the blood man's wife) with us and it was quite an experience. It was held in a community hall, which was absolutely packed with Saints of all ages and sizes when we arrived. We were directed up to the front where they were giving up the performers' seats for the audience - a mixed blessing as it meant we could see and hear what was going on which was more than most of the audience could do, but it was harder to get to the bar to help one cope with what one was seeing and hearing.

We had country and western, banjo and harmonica playing, joke telling and our lovely ladies of Longwood doing line dancing - at least two of them were under 40 and one or two were quite slim! They took it so seriously. I told you we needed the bar. There were a couple of drunks who regularly called out their opinions, especially when the sound system went down for the third time. Then there was the compere - a well known councillor who every now and again announced an item followed by ' ---that is if we can find them, they don't seem to be here at the minute!' This was all good fun and we felt we had had an interesting evening when the compere announced ' we now have Father Chris to sing a couple of songs before the interval.' You mean this is only half way through? You should have seen the look on dad's face! We managed two items after the interval then sneaked out as they were trying to fix the sound system (again) ready for the raffle. Some aspects of this island can feel very African.

After all that, we needed to prepare ourselves for the Chief Secretary's wedding and it was lovely. The cathedral was nearly packed and the bishop gave a good address. It does feel rather different when the couple are both divorced and have been living together for the last 4 years. Nevertheless it was extremely sincere, we sang lots of lovely hymns with Welsh tunes and the choir had worked hard for the anthem, which went very well.

Date: 7th December
To: Jon and Chinatsu
Subject: St Andrew's Day

Things are hotting up in more ways than one just at present. We have started all the usual things to do with the end of the Christmas term at school and today we had rather an unusual St Andrew's Day celebration. To start with St Andrew's Day was last Sunday but the ship was not in then so the celebration was delayed until the RMS was back from Cape Town. There were about 75 of us and we had a beautiful buffet lunch on board on the first day of really good hot sunny weather of this season.

There were plans for some Scottish dancing but we were all so full of food and alcohol and sun that chatting in good company on the sun deck was all that most could manage. A few people were ferried over to the visiting US navy support ship that has been visiting since last Monday. These ships are searching out suitable locations to be 'safe havens' for similar ships awaiting their next assignment or on route to their next support role. Not that easy to blow up a

US ship off Jamestown and judging how everyone knows everyone's business any shady stranger wouldn't have a hope of doing something unnoticed.

There were several of us who would like to have stayed on the ship and made our way back to UK for Christmas but I think we might have been noticed. What will you be doing for Christmas and New Year? I am so sorry none of us will be there. We really are a crazy family and do everything back to front what with us here and Beth and Olly out in Rwanda with Tim and Jo.

Date: 18th December
To: Beth
Subject: Disowned

I just bent down to pick up what I thought was an enormous dead cockroach when it waved a feeble feeler at me so - perhaps not - I'll use a brush! Thought I'd get you back into the Africa mode before you go.

We finished school on Tuesday and the 'Hosanna Rock' concert, which was in the cathedral, went very well. As I was asked to support the choir with the singing I got off very lightly and was spared that dreadful business of trying to keep all the kings, donkeys and sheep quiet in the vestry.

Now I have the painful job of telling my children that the next day my faithful husband of 34 years disowned me. In fact you probably would have too. The whole school (about 75) went down to the hospital at the top end of Jamestown, to start a parade of music and Christmas songs through the town. Everyone dressed up in cheerful clothes and bits of tinsel, including me. The teachers however also wore those funny glittery, tinsel type wigs - yes - mine was electric blue! and the darn thing kept blowing into my mouth when I was trying to sing, as it was quite windy even in town.

As we followed the pickup down the street, with its cheerful Christmas music blaring out, all the kids danced about and blew those dreadful party hooter things. We stopped every now and again to sing and collect money and people came to their doors and out of offices and shops to watch. When we passed the Teacher Education building there were all the students and staff looking over the wall – all except one. He was back in the staff room gulping coffee and hoping it would all be over soon and that no one would make the connection between him and the electric blue tinselled creature in the parade. We went down through town to Ann's Place and then at noon the buses collected us to take us up to Half Tree Hollow and the Rock Club for chicken and chips, ice-cream, music and skittles. We didn't escape from there until half past two when we put all the children on their buses for home. When I got back to Piccolo I went out on the golf course for a lovely hour of peace and quiet and no people!

Saturday was shopping. The ship was in for the second time in two weeks so there was fruit and veg in the shops again. Sunday was Jack's ordination (2 hours), Monday the staff dinner. Tonight we have choir practice then we are out to dinner, tomorrow there are carols and mince pies at Plantation House and on Sunday evening it is the island carol service outside the Court House in town. We have been invited somewhere for drinks on Christmas Eve before the midnight service. So you can see we have quite a lot to do. It is not the same as having family but we will be quite busy and it won't be as bad as last year. We will be having the Christmas meal at Mary and Bill's again, along with some others.

You however will be having a very different time. I hope everything goes well and that you both really enjoy it with Tim and Jo in Rwanda: I am sure you will. We will be thinking of you all - of that you can be sure. Take care and remember all the sensible, safe things you have learnt over the years when travelling in Africa and while you are there. We want you both back safe and sound.

Date: 22nd December
To: Tim and Jo
Subject: Marathon

Glad to hear that Beth and Olly arrived safely especially after all the different experiences that you two have had over the years on that route.

We are into the swing of various festivities with carols, cocktails and canapes, and things are a bit better as we now know more people. We are also a little more used to being on our own. Yesterday was quite a marathon, first Dad and I drove two cars to Rupert's Bay in order to leave one there. We then went straight on to church and as soon as we could escape we went along to Deadwood Plain and started walking up to Flagstaff. We were looking out for the environmental group who were walking up from Rupert's via the Boer Road and then down again via Sugar Loaf. This is one of the post box walks Dad had not yet got under his belt. They came up behind us so it all worked well and we had an excellent if fairly long walk including quite a scramble up to the top of Sugar Loaf, ending at Rupert's and the car. We got home about 4ish and then had to be down in town dressed in our black and white for the ecumenical carol service in the square at 7pm.

Am falling to sleep now so will wish you good night.

Date: 25th December
To: Tim, Jo, Beth, and Olly
Subject: Christmas Day

Happy Christmas to you all. We'll try and phone later if we can find the number! We had a very pleasant Christmas Eve at a party with champagne cup, smoked salmon and caviar; real candles on the tree and some carol singing. Our South African hosts brought things to an end in time for us all to get to the cathedral for midnight mass, which meant that it was past two o'clock before we crashed into bed. Slow start to the day, we looked at and listened to an excellent service from the united churches of Milton Keynes on BBC Prime (which is on one of our three channels over the Christmas holidays only, sharing with BBC World and the Discovery Channel).

Hope you all have a good day together, and best wishes for the rest of the holiday. We're off across the road now to Mary and Bill for Christmas dinner.

Love to you all from us both.

Date: 2nd January
To: Tim, Jo, Beth and Olly
Subject: Round and round

Best wishes for a very Happy New Year to you all. We played a round of golf, saw fireworks for the Sydney New Year celebrations on BBC World in the afternoon, and then went off for some dancing at the local Consulate hotel in the evening. It was reasonable but the live band only really had one type of music and one pace, which wasn't particularly fast - only loud! However we were there with a couple of pairs of friends and so we enjoyed ourselves and ended the evening by walking along the waterfront and then making a 'first foot' visit to the Scottish couple on the compound.

I broke a golden rule of mine for a dinner party the other day, that of not doing something I hadn't tried before, but I got away with it. We were out to lunch again on New Year's day and there is a dolphin trip tomorrow with about 30 others. I have never really experienced what people said about this kind of society before – that you just keep meeting the same set of people but in different locations. We did meet up with a few different people yesterday including the Governor and the doctors that we don't see so often. This was at the house of a couple who have just been working in Tajikistan - all sorts end up on St Helena.

I must tell you that Dad and I sang a duet twice in the last week. We were landed with this at choir one night when they were trying to sort out the Christmas programme. There is not much for soprano and bass and at short notice so we did 'Away in a manger' at the beginning of the midnight service from the back of the church, and as it sounded good the bishop wanted it again at the 'Nine Lessons and Carols' - but I think we will keep teaching as our day jobs!

Date: 8th January
To: Rosemary
Subject: New Year

Many thanks for your Christmas and other e-mail; it is good to hear from you. I do hope that you had a good Christmas and that you were able to have and enjoy all the family at least for some of the time. We sorely missed having some really good services here. We of course were on our own but this year was rather better than last year as we knew more people and so were invited out rather more. In fact we went to so many BBQs and cocktails etc that Richard and I really must do some serious exercise to wear off the additional pounds that seem to have appeared. One lovely thing was the Advent calendar that Beth sent to us. She and Olly had copied two A4 sized nativity scenes and behind each window was a photo of one or more of the family and close friends. It was a brilliant idea and gave us a warm feeling every time we looked at it.

Beth and Olly had an excellent time out in Rwanda as Tim and Jo tried to give Olly an introduction to the continent; celebrate Christmas in Kigali and then have New Year over the Ugandan border on Lake Bunyoni; followed by packing up their house in order to leave on 13th January. Beth and Olly (definitely impressed and with a greater understanding of Beth's love of Africa) are back home now but Tim and Jo are taking the long route home via Malawi and Zambia, Namibia and South Africa. They will then join the RMS St Helena and visit us for a week in March. Putting it like that it doesn't seem so long now.

Jon and Chinatsu on the other hand stayed in Farnborough, at least for Christmas but then it was decided that Chinatsu should have a trip back to Japan with Daniel in time for the New Year celebrations and then stay on for a few weeks. She really needs to get back about once a year to see the family and be in her own culture. In general she does love being in England, partly because of the independence and freedom from the traditional expectations that a young wife and mother faces in Japan. As this is a very busy time for Jon he won't feel it quite so badly and at least he will be able to catch up on some sleep as Daniel is still not that good at night. This is the long holiday here so I have another week before returning to school. The ship came up from Cape Town twice before Christmas and brought a fair selection of goodies. However at the weekend it will set off for Cape Town and then go on its yearly visit to Tristan da Cunha. I'd love to do that trip some day but as yet can't work out how to get the government to pay for it.

Date: 11th January
To: Jon
Subject: More socialising

How are you doing? I hope you are keeping yourself well occupied whilst the family are away. We had a very good dolphin trip last weekend. They were not jumping as much as when we went out the last time, but it was a lovely day and we had a very good time off Old Woman's Valley where we had an excellent swim and picnic. I even persuaded dad to play a round of golf when we got back in the afternoon.

The Education Department Day Out at the Blue Hill community centre at the other end of the island was an absolutely typical island affair. We were told it started at 10:00 so we arrived about half past and people were still arriving (there were about 160 altogether). Then everyone just hung around and chatted to everyone else because of course they all know each other very well. There were only half a dozen expats and it was nice being able to have a good chat with Saints. No activities had been organised so eventually some of the younger ones found a volley-ball kit, some others got out the skittle equipment for the skittle alley which is to be found in every community centre, others played cards. We eventually had an excellent meal - the highlight of the day - and then it was back to more chatting. So when a group set off for a walk we decided it was time to head off home as we had the car and the buses were not due to come until 5:00.

Last night was yet another dance this time the Friends of Guiding! It was most enjoyable and since 'King George' was playing the music was better than at New Year and there were some really lively numbers. I staggered up for golf yesterday morning so as not to disappoint Jill but I wasn't exactly at my best. Oh I forgot - I went to my first coffee morning on the island, there were about 20 people there and we had a good chat.

Date: 14th January
To: Beth
Subject: Advice

I have a few motherly words of advice for your teaching practice which you can ignore - at your peril:

- Keep a copy of everything – suddenly either you or someone else will want an obscure item and the last thing you want is to ransack your cupboards or, worse still, have to do what ever it is again at the last minute.
- Put off going out for a quick one with your mates until this 5 weeks is over: they will understand as your face gets increasingly more haggard.
- Get some sleep - the little dears have an amazing and uncanny knack of knowing when you are not quite on top, no matter how bright and cheerful you sound.
- All children are monsters with antennae a yard long to suss out every weakness.
- The alternative is to work in a government pensions office.

And now you can go off to prepare and I have a message for Olly
Dear Olly
   This is just a timely warning - IT CAN ONLY GET WORSE!
She is probably talking fairly rationally at the moment but will gradually descend into babble about QCA documents, literacy hours, attainment targets, tripartite planning, sub-levels, cognitive recognition, divergent thinking, strategies,

policies, IEPs, differentiation and much more. Just answer 'yes dear' or perhaps 'mm dear' would be safer. She will eventually not recognise you in the morning or worse still call you 'Dean or Justin or Ricardo or even Marlene' just answer 'mmmm dear, here is your caffeine supplement' and point her to the car.

When she comes to you at midnight and asks you to design a complete worksheet for Year 2 phonemes **don't** have a better idea of how it could be done! Just rifle through the huge pile of reference books scattered over her bed and floor and print out anything under the appropriate heading, remembering to put a space for name and class at the top of the page and a picture to colour.

If you ask her which Red Cross recruit should you send on a particular assignment do not be surprised if she replies 'I've got gym on Wednesday before lunch and have to photocopy the reading lists for Thursday morning and I don't know what to do about little Dougie who refused to be the dragon in drama this afternoon'. Red Cross probably isn't at the top of her priority list at the moment.

When she bursts into tears on Friday night just say 'mm dear' give her a big kiss and tell her she has got until Sunday afternoon until it all starts again! There again perhaps just give her a kiss. You have been warned. Thinking of you both.

Date: 25th January
To: Beth
Subject: Island in crisis

You are probably up to your eyes in preparation again this evening but we thought we'd send you something just to remind you that there is a world out there. In fact a very dangerous state of affairs exists at the centre of the universe.

We are indeed truly in crisis since the island is suffering simultaneously from diarrhoea and no beer!! These are not directly connected but indirectly they might be considered so, through Christmas and the ship.

Before Christmas the ship brought masses of fruit of all kinds and since we have a naggy consultant nutritionist on the island at present everyone has been eating vast quantities of fruit as they have been told it is good for them! Mind you, whether it is taken instead or as well as the normal diet is in doubt. It is also summer here so we have the local produce coming on line at the same time. Unfortunately all that fruit has to be eaten up fairly quickly as it is getting rapidly over ripe! With such an assault on the island digestive system, which is normally stuffed full of bread, chips and black pudding, all this fruit has had a fairly drastic effect hence the diarrhoea. That's the first problem.

For the second problem.... Well it appears that people are unable to drown their sorrows since everyone celebrated Christmas so fully and successfully that the island has run out of beer! (at least you cannot buy it in the shops, though most bars and clubs still have some so I am told). The ship isn't due in for another fortnight so hang on to that last six-pack. I told you it was a major crisis!

That said, there seemed to be enough drink flowing last night, although most of it was wine and whisky. We had the Burns' Night dinner at Ann's Place. There were about 75 people and, between the fish and the main buffet, guess who had been persuaded to sing a couple of Burns' songs - yes - your beloved (daft) parents. Mary couldn't get us any part music so poor old dad had to sing unison but persuaded me to sing on my own in one or two rather high sections. Father Chris played the keyboard as accompaniment (he also sang one himself). Very scary to expose oneself to lots of people one knows instead of an unknown audience.

This island seems to do funny things to one. Following our success at Burns' Night I came in a bar too early in an anthem I know well, at the patronal festival in the cathedral this evening - oh well - keeps one humble. Now I really must get back to my planning and preparation and check how my captured woodlice are doing.

Date: 30th January
To: Beth and brothers
Subject: Work and travel plans

My present contract ends on 27th August which, because of leave due, would probably mean that we caught the RMS to Cape Town on 1st August. We would then plan to see something of the world after our banishment here, which could be something like Jo'burg to Sydney, Auckland, Easter Island, Chile and home.

However the department of education would like me to stay another year, and from the pension point of view it would be useful and maybe relieve our children of some of the expense of caring for two old people in the future! The department has to have the support of the St Helena Government for the request to DFID. The process has started but I do not know when it will be definite one way or the other.

Mum has said, without the possibility of any negotiation, that if we are staying an extra year then she will be home for next Christmas as she refuses to contemplate another Christmas without the family. As I do not feel like sharing a cabin with anyone else again (especially three other men of whom one was drunk throughout) this means I'll be home for Christmas also. We reckon that we could take a proper leave this time, not the abbreviated version of last year. Either we would go round the world (RTW) clockwise in November/December with Christmas in UK and back to work soon after; or RTW anti-clockwise going straight to the UK for Christmas and RTW in January and back to work mid-Feb or so.

Time will tell and we will keep you informed of developments. Love to you all, Dad.

Date: 31st January
To: Beth
Subject: Pantos and things

Lovely to hear about all the things you have been doing in the classroom. The pantomime sounded great fun and just the sort of thing to unwind with. We have one here next weekend (Cinderella) and it is being put on by the crew of the RMS! This will be preceded by a variety of entertainment offerings from people on the island – songs, skits and an aged councillor as a stand-up comic!

Dad will have sent you the general information on our plans, such as they are. Things are going on much as usual at present and my mind has gone a complete blank as to what little titbit I can feed you to cheer up your day/night. I can see one looming on the horizon however. St Paul's school is putting on a fun event - a Valentine's Day special for all the family. For whom? Isn't that a contradiction? Mind you, on second thoughts, maybe it isn't on this island. I think Alice has me lined up to play the tambourine in a staff skiffle band!

When you have got over your fit of the vapours I shall bid you a sedate and composed goodnight, and wish you a pile of snow tomorrow so that you can have the day off on Monday.

Date: 2nd February
To: Beth
Subject: Choir Notes!

I have decided that it is time to give a closer picture of the inner workings of our church and choir. I compose these things while driving to work because the only thing on the radio is some fairly ghastly programme where Joe or Henry or Lillian or someone is putting on pop music for some request for an island person's birthday or whatever. Last time we heard that Joe had to do an extra shift on the radio station because Henry's daughter (aged 8) was having a birthday and he was expected to stay home for it! There is nothing secret on this island. The radio station is less than two hundred yards from my school which is on a hill and from which we have an almost 180 degree view of the Atlantic.

Back to the choir - the other week the choir mistress, who is also a deputy head at the secondary school and always appears a bit harried and somewhat disorganised (but is lovely), rushed in late as usual and scrabbled about trying to find some music- first in the jumble in a large box by the organ, then in the depths of the vestry somewhere. We finally settle down to sing 30 mins after given starting time at which point she says that the bishop hasn't contacted her yet but it is the patronal festival Sunday after next so can we look for some suitable hymns that we can pass by the bishop.

We sit there riffling through the index and try out one or two. The tenor who sits behind me and usually comes to practice has a lovely voice and good approximation to the notes though admittedly this is at the expense of the words which he just makes up. We try out some really dreadful thing which I pronounce as impossibly 'BORING' where upon the two dear sopranos go rigid in their seats in shock that I should dare to question the quality of church music. The three younger altos recover from my comment, collapse in giggles and agree it really is boring (aided and abetted by Richard who stands behind them). The choir mistress capitulates all of a fluster and we move on to another hymn, which she checks is to our liking. We then move on to the anthem choosing one that they have sung before since one week might not be enough to learn a new one.

Come Sunday (not the patronal one) we find the choir mistress is even later than usual, the bishop is in the vestry with the lay reader, choosing the hymns for this service. Two minutes later we are off processing in and with the bishop playing the organ perched on the organ bench (nothing if not versatile) in front of the congregation, in full regalia including his exceptionally tall mitre (under which by the way, he has his little cap thing which has a short tassle which sticks up and makes him look like one of the teletubbies - by his own admission). At this point the choir mistress rushes in and takes over at the end of the hymn. This gives her enough time to find out what the rest of the hymns are. My neighbour sometimes quite puts me off my stride as her accent is so strong I cannot recognise the words, then I don't know if I am singing the right verse.

Since I am at the back of the line leading in I have to concentrate for leading out as a week or two ago, when we had a full procession led by the Boys' Brigade band, the leading alto and I marched off down the aisle behind the band - then almost at the door turned to find the rest of the choir half way up the church being led at a very sedate pace by the crucifer, singing and trying to contain their mirth, followed by the bishop and clergy, who didn't seem to notice.

And so it continues – only today I was passing through the vicar's vestry to get to the choir stalls to deposit my collection (since I'm not very good at juggling my hymn book, a candle, my collection and my glasses case as well as sing, on the way up the aisle) anyway as I pass the bishop calls out 'Sue do you know this one?' So I go over 'Yes' I say, 'Good we'll have that for the processional then'. What can one say - they are very sweet people and it is an experience.

Date: 7ᵗʰ February
To: Rosemary
Subject: Mist and isolation

The mist has closed in once again and we can see no more than 50 yards so this seems a very good time to settle down to write an e-mail to you. The weather is probably equally depressing in your part of the world unless you are having one of those superb gales that are rather splendid to be out in, as long as you are properly dressed. As the saying goes, "there is no 'bad weather' only inadequate clothing". In fact the weather is all wrong here this summer and we have had wind and rain and mist almost non-stop and people are getting a little fed up.

Jill and I went out for a round of golf last Saturday as the mists were rolling in off the sea but we could see along the fairway at least as far as we needed to (that not being very far) so carried on. However the rain came and drove us in to the midway hut, then it lifted and after that it came again and we said 'to heck with it' and carried on absolutely soaked. What is it that makes one doggedly want to finish something instead of being sensible? Things were just a little better this morning though the tourists who were having their first look at the island during a ride in the charabanc probably didn't see too much.

Richard was down in town picking up the mail as the ship has been away for six weeks so we were hoping for a decent supply. In fact I think everyone was doubly pleased to see the ship as it has had nothing but trouble since it left here before Christmas. There was engine trouble on the way to Tristan da Cunha and when they arrived there the weather and swell were so bad that people were able to go ashore on only one of the three scheduled days of the annual visit. The ship returned to Cape Town and then a couple of days out they had engine trouble again. Since then it has been limping towards St Helena with everyone more or less holding their collective breath. She arrived, 24hrs late, very early this morning. A spare part is being flown out to Ascension Island. It is hoped that she will get that far before the other engine goes. You do really begin to realise how isolated you are.

Having said that, I have decided that there are three phases to settling on this island, at least as an expat. When you first arrive you spend the whole time looking seaward, thinking how big it is, how magnificent, how isolated the island, what marvellous colours and moods it has and almost all your attention is facing outwards with intense interest in the comings and goings of the ship.

In the second phase you begin to look inward as well, seeing how much of the island there is and all the different scenery and communities and what there is to do and get involved in, but you still look for and are conscious of the sea at every turn.

In the third phase you mainly look inwards, island concerns become important, the place gets bigger and you can go for stretches of time without being overly conscious of the sea. The ship is important for what it can bring in terms of people and goods and delays are a nuisance with ship's absences only important in times of personal/family crisis.

If there is a fourth phase then it can take two forms, either you become like the islanders and the sea is hardly noticed at all except by fishermen, with the ship a source of jobs, supplies and commuter transport to and from UK,

Ascension or Cape Town or, for those who stay a contract too long, it is keeping you prisoner and you are avidly looking outward again, anxious to sail away.

We felt the distance just recently though it wasn't too bad as Beth kept us informed and there were people to look after him but Jon had to be whipped into hospital. He had a perforated and gangrenous appendix apparently. He was operated on and Chinatsu and Dan jumped on the first plane home from Japan so were back before Jon was out of hospital. He seems very perky now and has the advantage of being able to spend time with the family after their time away. He will have to forego a trip to New York for work about which he was a bit disappointed but otherwise he is fine. Tim and Jo are in the middle of the Namibian desert heading in the general direction of Cape Town.

Date: 8th February
To: Beth
Subject: TV and circus at the cathedral

The stress - the strain - but we shall do it for our public - we must!! We are just recovering from an early morning service at the cathedral. Joy phoned yesterday (Saturday) about tea time, saying that she had had a message from the bishop asking if the choir would turn up for the 8AM service today as a TV crew had come off the ship and wanted to film a service at the cathedral. He said that this was the only time they could manage. Surprisingly almost all the choir turned up.

All the more surprising since the bishop put us through the mill last week with a service that seemed to include every conceivable fun and games in the book except incense (posh or ordinary) and the sleigh bells. It was Candle Mass - so we had candles; Presentation in the Temple – a procession of the whole choir and congregation; a psalm -

which had a descant we know but hadn't practised; and then a spontaneous rendition of some random 'Alleluias' by the bishop - who then wanted everyone to learn them led by the choir who hadn't been warned or prepared. Oh yes and there were three baptisms as well!

The weather has been very unusual lately. It rained over the whole of the Christmas holidays and has just carried on doing so and there have been some pretty strong winds as well. Friday and yesterday there was an almost island wide mist the whole day. The hot dry summer days just haven't appeared yet one can look out to sea and see the sun shining on a blue surface a mile or so out – weird. Well having had a chance to moan I had better get on to my least favourite activity and cook Sunday lunch.

Date: 15th February
To: Beth
Subject: Letting off steam again and Valentine's Day

That's it never again, not on this planet or anywhere else for that matter, not even if my life depended on it - I am not going to be part of a 'fun evening' for primary school children celebrating Valentine's Day - ever. Ridiculous! This whole island goes Valentine mad.

Dad and I got influenced by it to the point of writing a whole new radio programme late on Friday night looking into some of the romantic classical music we have on CD. That bit wasn't too bad. The ship had come in eventually, with a mountain of mail for us, which was great. Saturday I went with dad up to the radio station to do the programme that went out today. We went straight from there to South West Point, had a good picnic lunch and an excellent walk for about two hours. The weather was warm and sunny with a pleasant breeze. We got home just before six in time for me to gather my strength for the Valentine Ordeal.

The school has been preparing for this 'event' for about a fortnight. Staff decorated the community hall (not far from the cathedral) and got mountains of food and lots of music and all that palava, along with the usual fuss and bother. I didn't actually arrive until about 5 minutes before my absence would have been noticed. At the end of the children doing some general musical pieces, the Staff Skiffle Group had to do their piece. Yes you have guessed it - I had another go at the triangle! Alice was on the accordion, Gloria and Carolyn on guitar and the rest with shakers and tambourine but the hilarious bit was our IT chap on the bass. This was a tea chest and pole with a single string. The problem was that he has absolutely no sense of rhythm whatsoever. He would start this very obvious bass boom off more or less on beat but then he would slow down, realise he was out of time and so put in a couple of quick ones -- to catch up. I was standing behind him trying to put him right every now and again and desperately avoiding the music teacher's eye, as she was sitting the other side of the room in stitches.

When that episode was over things only got worse. There was a Master and Miss Valentine competition for the kids. I was supposed to help to marshal the little mannequins but luckily there were not too many of them and I was able to escape the embarrassment of the whole thing! Not that the doting parents and sundry relatives were embarrassed, they were lapping it up. But I wasn't finished yet, as the music struck up and chairs were moved to the side of the hall and the drinkers at the bar got themselves another round, I had to sell paper roses with little coloured ribbons, and balloons with valentine messages on. Come 10pm I'd had enough and escaped especially since I'd found out that the whole thing was scheduled to go on to midnight. The bishop, by the way, was in his element behind the bar! The children are only 7 to

11 years old and there is far too great an emphasis on 'lurrvv' and all that on the island as it is.

OK so I am a miserable old frump - now I have that lot off my chest I am feeling great. We had a lovely phone call from Jon earlier in the week just to let us know that he is fine and well after the op and he certainly sounded perky enough. The other thing is that the schedules for the RMS are out and we are planning when we can leave the centre of the universe and visit a few outer planets of civilization.

Date: 29th February
To : Rosemary
Subject: Christian in Distress

Lovely to hear from you. How encouraging it is that there seems to be such a thriving and growing youth group in the village at the moment. As for here, at least in our parish, there doesn't seem to be anything for anyone!! There is no Sunday school, no study group, no anything and although the bishop put on a video of the Alpha course last year this year there isn't even that. In Lent Richard and I look out for some sort of study/discussion group to go to.
Last year we went to the Baptists. The pastor and his wife are lovely people and the group (of about 10) was very welcoming but not really our thing. The pastor would preface his exposition with the ardent hope that we would have a really good and meaningful discussion on the subject after he had introduced it. I tried questioning some of his statements two or three times but after he had got over the shock that I was not just confirming what he said and following up with supporting comments (as his parishioners did) he firmly restated his position and quickly moved into a couple of closing choruses. A mountain of 'eats' was produced and probably an earnest prayer that this subversive voice would not be there for long. So what else?

There is the Salvation Army where of course we would get a good sing but probably a similar reception to that of the Baptists.

Then there are the Seventh Day Adventists. I heard their leader doing 'Thought for the Day' on the radio last week and he seemed to spend the entire time talking about what we could expect in the Next Life when it is how to live and deal with the questions provoked by this one that are more pressing to me.

Church of the Latter Day Saints? - move on.

Jehovah's Witnesses? (they have an enormous building called Kingdom Hall and one part of the island is almost entirely JW) - OK so I'm getting desperate. The reason why I haven't mentioned the Roman Catholics is because their sick priest went back to UK, they are down to 6 members and 4 of those are off island at present!

Maybe you might be able to send the odd notes of your study group occasionally if appropriate, there really is little here or at least not what I am looking for. By the way I started reading Brian Keenan's 'Evil Cradling' the other night, I am not sure how far I will get with it - I shall give it a good try.

I have just started half term so have plenty of time to get things ready for Tim and Jo who are coming on the next ship. They have had a wonderful time making their way south from Rwanda and have even managed to get their PADI diving qualification in South Africa during this last week so they hope to dive whilst they are here.

Talking of diving and such like, it was actually warm

enough for us to swim on Saturday so we took ourselves to the pool in Jamestown and had a good bit of exercise to work off the highly fattening bacon bun just consumed at the Coffee Shop. I couldn't find any green veg in the shops and many of the shelves were looking a little bare but a friend dropped in today with two pawpaws and some aubergines from someone's garden so that was a nice surprise.

Better stop and write my weekly e-mail to my offspring. I hope all the snow is more enjoyable than a problem. Thinking of you

PS I forgot the Ba'hai - but their lady on 'Thought for the Day' always sounds so doom laden and miserable!

Date: 7th March
To: Beth
Subject: Career change again

What a fantastic weekend with all that dancing at IVDF. It was probably just the thing after your hard work in teaching practice. I must admit my first reaction to hearing about your next Teaching Practice was Year 6? --- well I guess she can cope but after SATS and in the last term before they leave the school that is quite tough. You will have your ups and downs but it will be excellent experience.

The heading of this e-mail was not meant to be a hint to you but a reference to the new me! Now as you know I have been exploring which of my many talents I should offer to my adoring public. My career as a diva is still wobbling on (I sang one of the solo verses for our choir's contribution to Women's World Day of Prayer last Friday) and we did two radio broadcasts on the trot last Thursday. However I think perhaps, whilst my literary public wait for me to get over a temporary writer's block, I might turn to the long hair, ethnic muslin skirt and sandals brigade since my poor tortured efforts to express the essence of nature and the true message of the ultimate creation at the centre of the universe has been accepted for an Art exhibition. Or to put it another way the museum are putting on an exhibition of art and craft by people on the island and asked for contributions and my drawings of 'views from the golf course' were accepted. So there we go.

We are now looking forward to Tim and Jo's visit, which finally feels as if it is going to happen as they are on the ship now and are expected in only two days late.

Date: 11th March
To: Beth
Subject: Brother arrives

This is just a quick note to tell you that Tim and Jo finally arrived early yesterday morning (Wednesday, instead of Monday). The RMS first went to Rupert's Bay to discharge diesel (which is of considerable interest to us as the pumps ran dry about a week ago) and passengers were unloaded (sorry, disembarked) from there. We had the usual hanging around to get their cabin baggage, then came home about mid-morning. Love Mum

It was a beautiful, sunny day, the first after a couple of weeks of mist and rain. Accordingly, Mum took them up Diana's Peak, as we had planned to do that at the first good opportunity in case it went wet again for the rest of their stay. I had to do some work and then go into town to meet the two education visitors who also came on the ship (one for one day, one for a week).

Now they're off to the Napoleon stuff. Dinner party here this evening. All this food! Love from us all Dad.

****

What do people do all day on St Helena

PART THREE

Date: 22nd March
To: Jon
Subject: Mothering Sunday

Thank you very much for calling yesterday - it is some earthy person's law that says when you pop out for a walk for one half an hour in the whole afternoon that is when someone will phone. I am very sorry I wasn't in but really did appreciate your effort. I had an e-mail from Tim from the ship and a virtual card from Beth who had apparently also been trying to phone.

  The cathedral was almost full which was good and then we had a baptism and all the giving out of flowers besides a full communion service It was just as well that Father Chris was doing it so things swung along well and the sermon was literally under ten minutes.

  Thank you too for the lovely photo of Daniel, he looks absolutely great. Congratulations to you Chinatsu for getting the job at Heathrow. I hope that you enjoy it and that the travelling isn't too much. It will be lovely to get out of the house and have people to chat to apart from Daniel. The plans for moving sound very sensible and could be quite fun. That makes all three of our children looking for houses or flats in one year!! Your prowess with languages leaves me gasping already Jon, let alone aiming to get to translator status.

  We have had a really lovely time with Tim and Jo here. It was a big shame that they lost two whole days but everything seems to have gone right after they actually arrived. We had a nice mixture of showing them the island, providing various walking and climbing experiences, doing the Napoleon history bit, having a dolphin trip and a round of golf, and entertaining. We even had the governor and his wife for what turned out to be an excellent dinner party. The Governor and Tim could talk Foreign Office gossip to their hearts' content. Tim and Jo even managed to bring us a Mulanje Cedar chest (mini version) all the way from Malawi. That brought back some memories.

I returned to school today to recover!! Tim and Jo seem very relaxed and happy and ready for the next chapter of their lives. The sea was very calm yesterday and today so they are probably having quite a good trip up to Ascension.

The only other news is that the governor phoned me on Saturday to say that he noticed that I was not out playing golf as my Saturday partner has gone off on the ship so would I like to join him and the Chief Secretary next Saturday?!! I shouldn't make too much of a fool of myself (unless that aforementioned earthy person puts his oar in). Tim enjoyed having a go at golf but I don't think it was Jo's thing!!

Oh yes apparently we have a brand new shiny shower room downstairs at home in UK. The room has been virtually gutted (does that have a double meaning these days?) and a new shower, basin, loo, window, tiles and paint put in. Only hope it has worked - the agent is sending a photo.

Date: 31st March
To: Beth
Subject: League of Friends Derby

I am briefly toying with the idea of racehorse owner in my unceasing endeavours to find a job to get me out of teaching - oops there I go again undermining an eager young teacher trainee.

Friday night made up for what had proved to be rather a dire week of teaching. The League of Friends of the Hospital put on this 'Derby Night'. There were four races with six horses (of the hobby variety) in each. As I am on the committee I was throwing dice with Nicola to decide which horse moved and how far, and Dad was working the tote with Richard the bank manager, and another chap. Our Scottish neighbour was commentator and the young lady locum doctor was jockey for our horse. You could buy a horse for £5 and we called ours 'Symphony' by Beethoven out of Classic Mix. Examples of other horses were 'Chief Minister' by Budget out of Gladstone Bag and 'Bankrupt' by Credit out of Control (that one was owned by the bank manager). 'Dagga' by Weed out of St Helena was owned by the Chief of Police!!

In fact we won our race (all of £25) and one of the raffle prizes so we did rather well. It was only a shame that the number of people there was rather disappointing, there were too many other exciting things going on round the island! A return darts match between the Golf Club and the Police and a social at Kingshurst community centre, with the bishop behind the bar (until 3:00am so he said).

All this excitement was followed the next morning by me playing golf with the governor and chief secretary and I am glad to say that I did not make too much of a fool of myself. In fact, I beat one or other of them at several holes and did some really good drives. I am going out with them again this Saturday.

Dad is steeped in plans for our round the world trip home and surrounded by flight details, codes for airports, Rough Guides to everywhere and a bright shiny primary school atlas so that he can work out where everything is! We can be eating supper and watching the news, driving along to town, or tucked up in bed when suddenly he says 'do you think we should have two or three days in Easter Island?' or 'how far is Bondi Beach from Sydney?' As I'm surfacing in the morning he pipes up with 'do you think the flight into a sector counts towards the total number of flights for that sector?' while I am still groping for the tea.

Presumably all has gone well and you have picked up Tim and Jo and had a chance of a good natter to compare notes. It took some time to settle back into our ordinary routine after they left and I was even less keen on getting back to teaching, hence the renewed search for a career change. They are advertising for someone to work at the radio station but I rather think that they are looking for a Saint and I just can't do the accent!!

Date: 9th April
To: Tim and Jo
Subject: Wow!

WOW! You really have hit the ground running and everything seems to be happening. It sounds as if you have done well with the car although not quite like an estate when it comes to moving house. The house hunting seems to be very encouraging too.

By the way John Beadon phoned us up himself to ask if you were still on the island. He would like to have a really good chat with you (aside from the Saturday open house). I explained that you were back in UK so he asked if you were at work Tim, and I said yes so he thought he might phone you at the Foreign Office! We are going to his 94th birthday party on Saturday.

Last Sunday we learned that all these years Dad and I have been getting things wrong at Easter. We were reliably informed by the bishop himself, that, to quote him 'the three most important days at Easter are Maundy Thursday, Good Friday and Saturday Evening'. All this time I have been under the impression that the climax of the church's year was Easter Sunday - silly me. They are having the Easter vigil, Confirmation and 'Pontifical High Mass' at the cathedral on

Saturday evening as the main service, with just a said communion at 8am on Sunday. We have decided to desert the cathedral over Easter. We are concentrating on the local church with Father Chris, which had a quiet, sincere Maundy Thursday communion last night.

Off to Good Friday service now.

Date: 9th April
To: Beth
Subject: High Society

On Monday I narrowly avoided being appointed to some high office when I went to Plantation House after school for the AGM of the League of Friends. Quote by one member 'other people with jobs manage to be on special committees' to which I replied, 'Well yes, but they can slip in the odd phone call, or even get a letter written in office hours, whereas I can't even go to the loo except at 10:30 and a quarter to one'. Other people really have no idea, do they?

Anyway on Tuesday there was the grand opening of the art exhibition at the museum, which actually meant that all the contributors and the Governor and his wife turned up for a glass of wine and polite conversations about everyone else's work. I have to say all three of my pieces were on their own display board and not tucked in some dark and dingy corner. The trouble is I had to resist the terribly strong urge to stand in front of my own stuff and admire it saying to myself - there's a clever girl then.

On to Thursday when I was at Plantation House with the Governor's wife again (how I do hate those dreadful name dropping people always talking about who they know and who's had them to tea) - actually it was lunch this time. A 'thank you' to Mary for being chairman of League of Friends. It was a really good meal. In the evening we had a

Maundy Thursday night fish supper at Donny's instead of going there on Friday night.

As for the rest of the island, most of whom are out camping as far as I can gather, they must be having a very wet time as it is blowing great guns and has been tipping it down with rain on and off for two days now. It is a long established tradition to camp over Easter so I gather. A good many of them have probably crept back to the warmth and dry of home. After all it isn't exactly far! I presume all your job hunting and interviews are on hold over the holidays.

Date: 22nd April
To: Beth
Subject: The yachty and the old man

I'm glad the teaching practice went well and you had such a good report. What do you think of teaching that age group?

This has been quite a good weekend starting with a reasonable round of golf late on Friday afternoon and then a pleasant evening at Nicola's eating curry and meeting an interesting young South African chap who is sailing single handed round the world. He used to run a diving school in Mozambique but has only been seriously sailing for about 7 years. We went out to see his boat yesterday afternoon. It is just 26 feet long and really quite basic without masses of fancy equipment, just GPS and a couple of solar panels to help top up the battery. The rig was simple and seemed to require a fair amount of brute strength. The engine did start (when he decided to move anchor to put distance between himself and another yacht) but there was a fair amount of smoke! This chap was staying with the bishop who was also there on Friday tucking into curry, but in a fairly entertaining and reasonable mood. The only problem was that we left after midnight and the bishop, the yachty and the young locom doctor were still there two hours later. In the end the hosts had to tell them that it was time to leave!

On Saturday morning after my round of golf with Gill (not such a good one) we went to see an old man called John Beadon who is in his nineties and holds an open house on Saturday morning from noon to one when people drink beer and chat. After one has been invited once one can go any Saturday. He is an expat who retired to the island with his wife over 30 years ago, after a career with the Hong Kong and Shanghai bank, based mostly in Malaysia. He is remarkably with-it although rather deaf, so you can't have more than one conversation going on at once and you have to speak up. He heard our radio programme and phoned us up to invite us as he approves of Bach and Beethoven! We have been several times now. He lives in a pleasant house with a lovely garden up a track off the road we take to school. Needless to say the bishop is also usually there.

I must say it is the one time Dad and I catch up on the goings on and all the gossip of the island. You know that neither of us are any good at that – we never remember any of the juicy bits we happen to hear but old John likes to keep in touch.

Date: 21st April
To : Tim and Jo
Subject: Dad's 60th

I wonder how much 'gardening leave' as I believe it is called, you will end up with Tim, before they get things sorted at the Foreign Office. As for us we had a very successful 60th party for Dad at the weekend. Dad actually worked very hard collecting garden furniture from around the compound, rearranging our stuff here and then getting all the drinks organised. We had to be prepared for rain or sun as the weather has been fairly awful again recently. It was all mist and wind and rain on Saturday to the point that my golf with the governor was called off after two holes. However all dawned clear and bright on Sunday and Mary and Nicola arrived with crockery, glasses and the first of the four curries (cooked by Andrew) mid morning. This was my solution to the problem of no vegetables. Vegetables, especially the green variety, are not so crucial for curries. I had to give my friend eggs so that she could make the cake for me! We eventually had a great spread. I wasn't even too put out when the first guests arrived 10 mins before opening time.

We had over thirty adults and numerous kids who all seemed to occupy themselves racing round the compound and occasionally making a pit stop here for hotdogs and burgers. Madam Governor turned up fairly early and was in a good mood so that was all right. She had sent the Governor himself out to the HMS *Endurance* that had arrived in the bay a couple of days before, on his own! The atmosphere was pleasant and happy with drink flowing well but not excessively. Dad was very satisfied with the whole day particularly as he was then able to enjoy some of the newspapers that had come on the ship the day before!

Date: 26th April
To: Rosemary
Subject: Celebrations

It has been a good holiday with the focus being Richard's 60th birthday and searching for food! Well it was not quite that bad but the ship had been away for nearly 6 weeks and the shelves were looking very bare. It is not that we would starve but it was becoming very important to tap into the local exchange economy to avoid total boredom in the food line. Someone offered me broccoli and a cabbage a few days ago - yippee GREEN vegetables. There has not been a hint of them in the market. Goodies are now in the shops as the ship came in at the weekend. Our children phoned for the birthday of course and one was again so thankful for the contact that a phone link provides – even more immediate than e-mail.

After a shuttle up to Ascension the ship was due to leave for Cape Town yesterday with a number of friends and acquaintances and so the week seemed to fill up with farewells of one sort or another. This weekend was my birthday so more phone-calls from the children - lovely. I hope to do some more drawing this holiday as well as putting together another radio programme and trying to write a piece about what people on the island do all day. I remember it being one of the things we wanted to know after looking at the official video, and tourists frequently ask the same thing. Mind you, even after spending 18 months here I'm not sure I have the answer!! The latest ship brought a number of parish magazines so it was very nice to catch up on the goings on at home.

Date: 28th April
To: Christine
Subject: Heart attack

My brother has sent an e-mail telling us of Pop's heart attack. He gave us a phone number for the hospital but given our situation I thought it made more sense to keep in touch through you and him. Simon said no more than that the doctor said that Pop was likely to be in for 3 or 4 days and that the symptoms were much like the stroke he had before. Please tell him that I have been in touch and am thinking of him and hope that he recovers soon and give him my love.

Unfortunately the island is going to be without power all day tomorrow and on Friday so that they can deal with a rockfall that threatens the power station. However power will be restored each evening so communication should not be affected too much and of course the telephone will still be on. It is in these situations that one suddenly feels the distance and the lack of air access. We have a high powered team of people from DFID and the Foreign Office out here at the moment discussing the on-going saga of air access and getting precisely nowhere - and we think bureaucracy and decision making is slow in UK.

Date: 9th May
To: Rosemary
Subject: Disaster and Music

There was a bit of a disaster last week. The valleys are so steep and rocky here that they are vulnerable to big rockfalls, especially after heavy rain. Since the single small power station is situated at the bottom of one of these valleys this is rather important. To avoid an accident, the valley sides are checked regularly and it was decided that a controlled rock fall should be carried out to shift unstable rocks. They shut the power station down so it could be evacuated during the operation and got on with the job of dislodging some rocks which would then roll down and dislodge any other dodgy ones. It was announced over the radio that it would last only two days and power would be back in the evenings.

Well after three days of no power people were rather fed up. Everyone had just stocked up their freezers from the last ship's visit and there it was all going off!! Power was eventually restored and now everyone is wondering how much of the food they dare to eat. Being islanders they will probably eat it all!! Also, on one part of the island, a lot of Cable and Wireless stuff was ruined by rocks. Heyho all part of life's rich whatsit...

I did enjoy putting together our last music programme. I decided to try and keep off our favourites of Bach, Beethoven, Mozart and Monteverdi and give a few others more of a look in. I discovered a fantastic trumpet CD which had come with the BBC magazine. There was also another one called 'Forbidden Music' by Czech composers who had been sent to camps in the war. When the ship comes in from Ascension it brings all the accumulated post, sometimes from as much as six weeks and it is a real bonanza as we suddenly have huge piles of Economists, Music, Wildlife and Literary magazines to feast on. It is then also that you realise what a limited view we get of what is going on in the world even from our dear old BBC.

All is relatively calm on the church front as the bishop has gone off island. We have Father Chris and Brother Jack at the moment and they seem to be coping very well. Chris called in the other day for tea and to unwind. He is a clever, well-read musician who used to teach (as a Brother) in a boys' prep school before coming here and being ordained. He works incredibly hard. Jack is very different though equally hard working - older, more everyday and a solid, salt of the earth type with a Saint wife who is lovely. We have about 5 more weeks before 'himself' returns no doubt very full of his private audience with the pope about which he was very excited before he left!

Date: 15th May
To: Beth
Subject: Present and future!

The ship came in yesterday bringing with it my birthday present. I love the cover of the journal and am determined to keep it up once we are on our RTW trip. Dad is having another push at trying to get some sense out of the travel agent in South Africa but it is a bit of an uphill job.

We seem to have had lots of visits by ships of one sort and another just recently and there has been a DFID team out here for a couple of weeks. Dad did get a chance to talk to one of them. Unconnected with that we have just had confirmation by e-mail that we have been given our extension. All the more pennies in the pension pot and a sigh of relief by the offspring.

There is nothing of major excitement to report about life at the centre of the universe (is that a contradiction do you think?) except to say that it has rained most of the week, I survived the first week of teaching this term, the island ran out of onions and eggs, and tuna is on the menu for breakfast, lunch and tea.

I think it is time for another special.

A SPECIAL
Ship Ahoy!

The town was buzzing, with all and sundry busily trotting up and down the main street. People carrying plastic bags advertising the two 'supermarkets' in town, bulging with--- well I'm not sure what unless it was fish and pork or perhaps lettuce which had just been bought in from the country. There was definitely a good mood as everyone stopped to chat to everyone else that they hadn't seen for at least two days. Yes - the ship was in. The bishop, in very casual attire topped by his well worn sun hat, rigorously asserted that he had been taken quite by surprise as he hadn't realised that the ship was in today since he had given up having his life ruled by the ship ages ago! Well maybe he hadn't run out of potatoes, onions, eggs or milk and his garden was keeping him well protected from the total lack of fresh fruit and most vegetables in the shops, and his car didn't need a replacement for a blown cylinder head gasket. Then again, perhaps this time he was not saying farewell to or greeting any of the ship's human cargo.

Unlike the bishop, a good percentage of the population are only too aware of the ship's schedule and it is difficult to overstate the impact and importance of the ship in their lives. Even many of the old people who have never wanted or felt the need to leave the island in 80+ years wait in anticipation or sadness as the ship brings sons, daughters, grandchildren and friends - or takes them away. The RMS, staffed largely by Saints, brings household freight, business goods and hard stores from UK, carries mail from Ascension Island and fresh goods, clothes, general freight, mail and diesel from Cape Town.

Then there is the annual trip to Tristan da Cunha with the Governor and his wife on board. RMS passengers include Saints, expat contract personnel and tourists.

Tourists are either on 'the holiday of a lifetime', or 'yet another cruise but something different', or 'an adventurous voyage', or 'a Napoleon pilgrimage' or 'a trip to see the next strange place the family has chosen to work in'. For them the life at sea with deck quoits, shuffle board, skittles, quizzes, beef tea mid-morning, daily noon bulletins (including the information that there are 4000 metres of sea below the ship), whales, dolphins and albatrosses, good food and an e-mail facility, is as important as the destination.

For contract personnel it is the only way to get to the island but who's complaining since the contract starts at departure from UK. To the Saints however, the RMS is commuter transport albeit with more food, comfy chairs and a somewhat longer journey time. It takes them away to more lucrative work on Ascension, in the Falklands and in UK. It takes them on shopping trips and medical visits to South Africa. For a Saint to accompany a member of the family or a friend on a 5 day trip to the Cape with a two day hospital stopover and a 5 day return is not uncommon. It also brings Saints for family visits, a house building expedition or a final homecoming.

The RMS is not the only ship that visits of course. There are the cruise ships – floating towns and cities – that offload hundreds of passengers via their small boats - if the ship's personnel consider it calm enough. This decision is sometimes at odds with that of the local Authorities who, it appears, are not allowed to use their expertise to get the visitors ashore. The visit of a ship such as the QE2 engenders great expectations. Drivers take out special taxi insurance for the day, extra food is prepared in the several eating places and stalls are laid out up on Longwood Green near Napoleon's Longwood House. The (1927) charabanc is brought out.

All day groups of tourists are to be seen being ferried between the various historical sites associated with Napoleon, slave trading and the defence of the island by the British in days gone by. Some might also fit in a round of golf on a course that might leave something to be desired in quality, but will have few equals when it comes to splendid views. There is considerable frustration and disappointment, not to say loss of revenue, should the conditions be deemed too rough for disembarkation.

Whilst in school one morning, pupils and staff of St Paul's heard a loud noise above the buildings. Upon investigation there, hovering overhead, was a helicopter from the visiting SA Navy destroyer. It made its presence felt again with what seemed like an invasion during a church service but it was only delivering guests for Sunday lunch at nearby Plantation House. In fact the ship's chaplain was in church dressed in smart white tropical uniform and delivering the sermon. The ubiquitous helicopter could be seen once more by those settled in at Donny's, as it executed the most delicate landing on the narrow waterfront, like a butterfly negotiating a visit to the smallest of flowers.

Then there are the yachts. St Helena is a popular stopover for the wide variety of yachtsmen who traverse the

Atlantic or who are making their way between South Africa and Europe. The island thus echoes its historical role as a port in which to stock up on water and supplies. Occasionally these visitors are enticed to stay for several months.

The island of course has its own boats for fishing and for pleasure. An excursion out to see the dolphins (and possibly to glimpse a whale!) combined with a picnic and a swim off Lemon Valley, is a very special occasion.

However most of the time, when you look out to sea and watch the sun sparkling on the water or the storm clouds gather and roll in across the waves or the moonlight playing over the ink black surface, at least as an expat, you are conscious of being on a very small island in a very big and seemingly empty sea.

Date: 18th May
To: Beth
Subject: School - ugh!

I can imagine the frustration about not quite getting the job when there was no obvious reason why not. However the gender factor can be quite strong in a primary school. They are often looking for men but can't say so. Your present school sounds really dire. I hate shouting too and get very cross with myself if I find I have been forced into it. The best thing is that you can start afresh in a new place after this and no one will know that you ever shouted.

Teaching isn't that bad - honest - you don't have to cycle on a motorway as the only way out! Cycling sounds a good idea and helps one's figure as well as fitness, unless one stops off for a burger and fries on the way back of course, or the St Helena equivalent - a tuna fishcake in a bun.

Nothing to report here except that we have a three and a half days in school this week as it is Ascension Day and then St Helena Day on Friday. Then there is Whit Monday followed by the Queen's Birthday on the following two Mondays. That's one way to survive. For some reason that I haven't quite worked out, I found myself volunteering to be one of the cooks of pancakes on the League of Friends stall on St Helena Day. I must be mad or perhaps this place just gets to you in the end.

Date: 22nd May
To: Beth
Subject: Interview and pancakes

Brilliant! Well done on getting another interview. You didn't say what they had asked you to do as your party piece. Now just make sure you don't go to bed too late on Sunday night, and remember to brush your hair, clean your shoes, change your knickers ---- what a good thing I am a long way away and you can't throw anything at me.

It has been a good week this week as I had no lessons on Thursday because we took the school children to church for the Ascension service and then had the afternoon off; then yesterday was St Helena Day. Dad and I had a lie-in but then I had to get down to the waterfront with all my gear for making pancakes with Nicola. We thought we would be doing it from 2 to 4, but somehow things changed as they do and I was there from noon to nearly 6 cooking pancakes. I quite enjoyed it and I was a real wizz at making pancakes with two frying pans on the go at once for some of the time!!

The Saints gradually congregated down in the town and in the Mule Yard and Waterfront as the afternoon wore on. I now recognise a lot of faces and chat to many of them. There were a few stalls scattered around as well as ours, mostly producing food. A mini marathon was organised as well as some water sports and a small parade with Miss St Helena and a band or two but for the most part people just seemed to wander round, eat and watch and eat and chat - oh and eat. Then in the evening it was dancing in the MuleYard for over 40s and dancing at Donny's for the under 40s. We came home once Dad's stint on the Gate was over. It was generally a good day.

Today, apart from golf, we have had a quiet time with Dad enjoying himself exploring all the possibilities and impossible combinations as we try to fit in Perth, Alice Springs, Cairns, the Great Barrier Reef, Sydney, Auckland, Tahiti, Easter Island, Santiago, Tierra del Fuego and UK. That's just for leave, you ought to hear what we are planning for the end of the contract!

Jo looks as if she is going to enjoy her new job with Christian Aid and Tim starts his on Monday, the problem consular cases for the Far East I think.

Date: 26th May
To: Beth
Subject: Life Processes

Came into school the other day when I was greeted by a tug on the arm by little Anwen (girl) from year 3 'I'm sorry Mrs Fisher but I forgot to bring my sperm in today' - 'Oh er did you Anwen well that's a shame. Do you think you could bring some in tomorrow and we can put it in the fish tank and watch as the tadpoles hatch.' We are doing Life Processes!

Date: 5th June
To: Beth
Subject: Earthquakes and American invasion

When the ship went up to Ascension just recently, it had to sit around off shore unable to get any passengers on or off. Apparently the swell was such that it was not safe to try and get anyone down the ladder and on to the local water taxi! They had to wait two whole days before things calmed down. They even went round to English Bay to see if they could land the passengers there. We heard one explanation that it was due to an earthquake under the ocean to the north of Ascension but haven't had that confirmed. The RMS returned on Friday and set off again the same day for its penultimate trip to UK. They are planning to keep it in the southern ocean from then on and not all the Saints are happy as that would mean no one could go all the way to UK by sea.

      The other shipping news is that we have an enormous American supply ship anchored off here at the moment and she is due to stay for about a month. Apparently we have been designated a 'safe haven' for the supply ships contracted by the American navy. This one has an entire field hospital, food and water supplies for an advance marine force and goodness knows what else aboard (we did wonder whether she might quickly build the airport whilst she's here!) Apparently she roams around the Atlantic waiting to be called in when the Americans decide to march in and solve all some poor country's problems. Perhaps I should have put this last paragraph in code in case a terrorist organisation is peeking into my e-mails.

      Your school does sound rather horrendous but I pray that the last week goes well. Talking about praying - the bishop is back!

Date: 13th June
To: Beth
Subject: QBP again

Well done over your essay as an example of excellent work - I told you that people who could both do science and write decent English are a rare breed these days! I'm glad that another interview has come up, partly because it gets you off teaching another day

Well done also to Olly for doing so well over finding the flat though I am disappointed to think that you don't intend to wash for a year. As for other activities associated with bathrooms I don't want to know, but feel it incumbent upon me to tell you that in Bristol they have moved on from the Middle Ages - can't speak for Devon as I don't know enough about the customs down there! Seriously though, we are delighted that you have found somewhere even if the bathroom arrangements are strange. We are looking forward to seeing it when we come in December.

The last of the run of special holidays is tomorrow - the Queen's Birthday has arrived again. I am not sure why we have the day off since we actually had the QBP yesterday. There was the usual large marquee over the car park area in front of Plantation House and a long queue of cars arrived at noon. Everyone, dressed in their best, shook hands with a helmet of swan feathers and moved swiftly on to the drinks.

The next two hours were spent drinking steadily (95% of the people making a real effort to help the governor use up his alcohol stocks before he leaves) and talking to any and everyone at random, knowing that it didn't really matter what they said as the band, though good, was so loud that no one could hear anything else. Mind you this had its dangers as every now and again the band suddenly stopped for reviving liquid refreshment, and you found yourself in the middle of a sentence in a conversation about which you hadn't a clue and everyone could hear you. Very disconcerting - have another gin and tonic. 2:00pm came and the purple clad bishop wearing his matching teletubby hat departed, and everyone else then staggered off as well.

      This morning Dad and I played golf with the governor and none of us was quite playing to our best. Which was a bit annoying for me since I, at least, was one of the 5% not trying to empty the cellars the day before. By the way, the young priest has also got himself a teletubby hat only his is black and he wears it when not wearing the one that looks like the top of the black queen in a chess set (I think that one is called a biretta or is that a type of hand gun?).

Date: 27th June
To: Jon and Chinatsu
Subject: Across the island

We have started the week rather dramatically as there was an organised walk today which went from one end of the island to the other along the longer dimension. It started near us above Prosperous Bay Plain, where the government plan to think about the possibility of considering the feasibility of suggesting a tentative plan for idea of an airport - maybe! The route then climbed up towards the main peak but skirted round half way up and then carried on to the other end finishing at South West Point 15miles away. That is not bad considering that the island is only 9x5 as the crow flies. Dad did almost all of it and I did the first bit that I hadn't done before and joined in again after the party had done the peak part. I am no longer so keen on walks that include near vertical inclines (well that's what it feels like). We finished just before the end as we were well behind the rest of the group (mostly islanders, who all seemed horrendously fit) and had had enough.

Dad is mulling over different parts of our holiday plans and suddenly bursting out with 'shall we take 2 days in the Blue Mountains and go straight there from the airport?' or 'what do you know about Rio?'

Look after yourselves, we think of you very often even without the prompt of all the photos that we have posted in every room.

Date: 30th June
To: Rosemary
Subject: Murder!

You and the vicar really are going to be busy with so many more churches and parishes between you. The bishop here has got one priest, a deacon and 5 lay ministers to help him and a total island population of around 4000. I am not sure that it is in the rule-book that he has to spend every Friday afternoon and evening down at Donny's on the Waterfront but it could be argued that this is where he meets the people. Still I am trying not to get at him all the time and that is best done by not thinking about him at all.

It must have been fun, if exhausting, with the grandchild. Did you find that she took longer to start talking in the first place although she now manages to jump between three languages? I once heard someone talking about the multilingual situation for young children and the gist of it was that the child has a lot extra to sort out and digest so doesn't always get started so quickly. Our grandson Daniel is talking (after a fashion) both Japanese and English so Jon tells us. I have always been completely useless at other languages and it has been just as well that we have worked mostly in Commonwealth countries so there has always been English of some sort. I have become very adept at translating local versions. I am not sure how we will be getting on in South America when we visit, as neither of us have the slightest idea about Spanish or Portuguese. Even here the language needs a certain amount of interpretation it having some very strange 18th century constructions and odd vocabulary, apart from the strong accent.

Richard is deep into the planning of our leave at the moment. We will set off from here at the end of October and go by a somewhat circuitous route to UK arriving 10 days before Christmas. I stated my conditions and said that the only way I would do an extension on St Helena was if we could have Christmas with the family, So if plans work out we will be going to South Africa (of course), Australia, New Zealand, Easter Island (I've always fancied that), Chile - including going down to Tierra del Fuego, a brief stop in Rio and finally to UK. Just at the moment our house is wall to wall Rough Guides and Lonely Planets.

One rather sad thing happened recently which you wouldn't expect in such a community as this. We have had a murder! It seems that a 19 year old was in a fight with a couple of other young men down on the Waterfront one Friday night. On the following Monday the chap's body was found in the dry moat area between the Waterfront and the swimming pool. It appears that there was rather a lot of drink involved. As you can imagine everyone is very shocked especially the three families. Just when you think that this island at least, avoids the sort of violence found in the West something like this happens. Forensic specialists are coming on the next ship.

The problem of drink is really a very serious one here (particularly amongst the young) but up to now there seems very little real will on the part of the Saints to tackle it - they seem to be rather fatalistic. Although I think a few are starting to think about it.

Beth is finding that jobs are not at all easy to come by. She keeps being told that she did a very good interview and has excellent rapport with children and that she shouldn't change anything but no, not this time.

Don't work yourself to a standstill, make sure you take time out in that lovely garden of yours. I shall look forward to seeing how things are going on even if it is in the middle of winter by then.

Date: 18th July
To: Jon and Chinatsu also Tim and Jo if you are sharing the house by now!
Subject: Cook in chief and tortoise creation

Daniel will presumably think he is in seventh heaven with 4 people to entertain him and take him out and generally be there to boss around. Hope it's going well.

In the meantime I have been excelling myself in a field that does not come naturally, as you all know only too well. I set up a farewell dinner party last weekend for our very good friends who were leaving. It started out as a sensible seven, but by the time the people all turned up (did I mind but he/they are house guests?) it was ten! - Was the cook of the year fazed? - perish the thought and peel a couple more potatoes and a carrot. It did all go very well and the food was both good and sufficient thank goodness!

Then this weekend your father had invited a couple of families and associated visiting grandparents to climb Flagstaff followed by high tea - that made fifteen! Great - oh yes the family with three children were all vegetarian! HELP - answer - beans, corn pie, savoury rice, cheese and onion quiche and lots of ice cream all of which are available at the moment. It has taken all of today for me to recover.

Prior to the family invasion I had forsaken my golf on Saturday morning in order to create a tortoise -- sad isn't it. The doctor's wife is a potter and she invited the League of Friends ladies (who raise money for the hospital and other causes) to come and do some potting and make a tortoise for each of ourselves, and one for the governor's wife as a farewell present to remind her of Jonathan, the 200 year old tortoise which lives in the grounds of Plantation house. (Weird to think that he could have looked Napoleon in the eye – on the other hand I don't think Napoleon was partial to crawling around on the ground.) Though I say it myself my creation turned out very well and I was chosen to do the design on the shell of the gift one. A new career - probably not enough demand to warrant giving up my day job just yet.

Date: 31st July
To: Tim and Jo
Subject: Homesick and Houses

I'm very glad to hear that the house seems to be moving on at last and that an actual date might soon be agreed. Your job in the Consular section sounds interesting Tim. I'd love to have a good chat and hear more about it. Very satisfying when things work out and I guess China could be one of the more difficult places to deal with.

    I felt decidedly claustrophobic and homesick this afternoon. Two years is definitely long enough in this place. There is no opportunity to work and act to one's full potential and reining in all the time is very unsatisfactory. I can do the teaching standing on my head - in fact I do sometimes but the sad thing is that they don't even notice!!

    Why are we doing an extra year? - well there is the pension, another year's salary and then of course we do end up with two round the world type holidays instead of one. I just have to keep remembering that and we have just received the Lonely Planets for Mongolia, Beijing and The Trans Siberian Railway!

Very many thanks for the newspapers of whichever persuasion and day, with or without coffee stains. They are truly appreciated with your father wearing a grin from ear to ear and a distracted look in his eye. Even I now sit for hours reading them and getting in touch with somewhere else and a wider range of thought patterns.

Date: 1st August
To: Rosemary
Subject: Families

You certainly seem to have been very busy but how lovely to have the family down from Scotland. I am really missing ours at the moment - they seem to be in the middle of all sorts of changes and so on and we are stuck way out here.

I should think by the time we do finally settle back home we will find much has changed as far as the church is concerned. It is just as well we will be visiting this Christmas so we will be able to catch up; I am really looking forward to that in all sorts of ways. I am refraining from saying anything about the bishop, and the very unsatisfactory situation at church here, as it does no good to complain and it does make us work a bit harder for ourselves. I sat in the pew this morning and there in my mind once again was the TV picture of a woman in one of the refugee camps in Dafur, just sitting looking defeated, with nothing and so alone. It is so often the women in those situations who bear the most pain, isn't it?

This is a bit of an up and down e-mail so far - sorry about that. Just a touch of frustration creeping in when generally we are doing well and I for one had some excellent SATs Science results at school to celebrate last week besides achieving several decent scores in golf!

Tim and Jo are almost at the point of getting a moving date for their house and Tim sent a lovely cheerful e-mail being pleased about work and solving some consular problems long distance with the Chinese. Having put in a new kitchen with the help of his friend, Jon is now tackling the bathroom, which badly needed doing! All we need now is for Beth to overcome the problem of the dearth of jobs in the Bristol area at the beginning of next term and everyone will be well away!

Date: 8th August
To: All in Tardis No 47
Subject: Exciting life

Hi everyone - this is to assure you that I am in a much better mood than I was when I wrote the last e-mail. Firstly thank you very much Jo, for news especially about the job and also the encouraging stuff about the house. Secondly thank you all for the steady supply (ship allowing) of mail and papers that come through. Dad is on tenterhooks waiting for the phone call to say that the post has been sorted and is ready for collection every time the ship comes in. (He goes down to the Castle and in by a back door so that he can get it the same day as it arrives even if it is weekend or after office hours.) Apart from mail we seem to have had quite a changeover of personnel with a number of new people coming in on the ship and not a few finally getting off the island - I didn't put it like that - did I?

The request for purchase of our tickets has been made and agreed and we are hoping that the tickets themselves will be on the ship when she comes up from Cape Town at the end of the week. Until the ship comes our thoughts have jumped a year and our noses are now buried deep in the Trans Siberian Railway and Russia - truly scary stuff. As dad says never mind the language, they don't even have the right script - which, as far as I can see, means that even if we do pick up a host of leaflets we won't even know if we have the right ones let alone what they say. Besides all this - you know my problem with not being able to tell right and left - well all the Lonely Planet literature etc seems to go from left to right ie Moscow to Beijing and we want to go the other way round. I could be stranded on the wrong platform for years waiting for a train in the wrong direction.

Back to Saint Helena where you can't get lost however hard you might try. Life is about as exciting as always - we have such an enticing list of events going on here that it gets harder and harder to choose: late night shopping at Spar on Fridays; watching people getting on or off the ship once a fortnight or so; the Longwood Girl Guides coffee morning on Wednesday; and the Blue Hill dance on the last weekend of every month.

Actually I have enjoyed this last week as there has been stormy weather for about 5 days now. There have been gale force winds for much of the time and then waves of torrential rain or swirls of particularly thick and wet mist sweeping over the island at regular intervals. I love it like that though the temperature has been rather cold especially over at St Paul's. Messes up one's golf rather but we get fabulous cloud formations to look at instead.

Date:15th August
To: Beth
Subject: Music Festival

We certainly are having winter this year. It has been blowing great gales again and it really has been cold, at least up here in Piccolo and over at school. The children sit in lessons with their coats on and I have several layers as well. Never mind, it has not stopped us going out to various activities this week!

We have been having a Music Festival week. The old instruments and equally old players on Monday were quite interesting and there were a surprising number of different instruments including mandolins and old accordions. Tuesday we had the Ladies' Orchestra. I must say that I was quite impressed as the variety of instruments had improved from last year and they had done so much rehearsing it was bound to be better. The only problem was some of the soloists were not really ready for that role yet! – one or two of the singers though were excellent. Next up the combined Primary schools concert - a marathon but a good one. It was nice to see so many learning new instruments - there is not the peer pressure to give up these things here on the island as there is in UK.

We passed on the Secondary School's talent competition; after all there is a limit to what we can stand and loud pop music and out of tune, badly articulated groaning about 'lurrrv' was more than we could take! The Infant schools combined production 'Noah' aaaahh! Very good, extremely slick with each school slotting in with their part very well and every child knowing exactly what they had to do. The 'ark' had been built by the prisoners at the jail, though there was some dispute about terms and conditions with that at one stage! The Pilling School effort at putting on the 'Lion King' was errr commendable!

The week concluded with an entirely unrelated event; that of the League of Friends Casino night at Plantation House again. It was an excellent evening and since the crew from the ship ran everything there was little for committee members to do. That was just as well in my case as we had a puncture on the way over and it was pitch dark. There we were all dressed in our best, up on the narrow lane above Hutts Gate just where the wind blows over the ridge, with no streetlights of course and the batteries dead in the torch! I stood with my lovely blue pure silk kaftan flapping in the breeze, holding greasy wheel nuts while Dad managed the change. He was OK until it came to lining up the wheel nuts on the new wheel so it was just as well another car eventually turned up. When we finally arrived Her Graciousness was standing on the steps of Plantation House greeting everyone and all I could do was wave two oil-covered hands and request to be led to the nearest loo.

Only other happening of note was that the governor went into hospital the morning after we had played golf with him. The poor chap is getting somewhat worked up about leaving and all that involves and his blood pressure shot up. They let him out to play golf with us again on Saturday so perhaps we were not the cause! He was much better when we visited the hospital after church today.

Date: 24th August
To: Beth
Subject: Another new career option

You are now being addressed by the Managing Director cum Artistic Coordinator cum Resident Artist of 'Viewpoint Publications SH'. Assets - one completed and published cartoon, four landscapes under publication and a second cartoon on the drawing board, sales - yet to be confirmed, (that is I haven't checked up with Edith as to whether any of the cards put on sale in the museum last week have actually been sold!) profit - 75% of sales when they occur! Oh the pressures of business - you have no idea.

Well at least it has kept me sane! I couldn't wait to get to the end of term this time. There is the big build up (at least in the year 6) to the SATs and then what seemed to be an interminable period when I couldn't get on with things properly as the children were constantly being pulled out for music practice, including tambourine routines, rounders and football tournament practice and then end of term performances. I used to really enjoy all that sort of thing but I must be getting old. However my year 6 had excellent results again, which was very satisfying, good for the children and it proved to these somewhat suspicious Saints that this expat does know what she is doing!

Now it is a case of catching up on e-mails, planning at least two radio programmes, looking up somewhere to stay and what exactly to see on Easter Island (the tickets have actually arrived so it looks as if we really are going). As from September, Cable and Wireless are planning to reduce the 'on-line' rates to start from 9pm instead of 10pm which will mean that at last we can get to bed earlier or more likely that even more time is spent on line! However it is still dial-up and not broadband.

I hope that the move went well and that you have been able to get all Tim and Jo's stuff over to them. Now we are looking forward to seeing their house in December.

Date: 25th August
To: Tim and Jo
Subject: Not long now

Well I wonder how many boxes you have left to unpack. If it is anything like us you get most of them done but it is the last two or three that seem to hang around and they are the ones with all the bits and pieces that you didn't know where to put in the last house either!!

It is end of term here and everyone is tired. The problem is that the only holiday the teachers get between the end of one school year and the beginning of the next is two weeks! I have just heard that a newly qualified teacher (mother of 2 children) who has been with us less than a year has resigned. I reckon that if they don't do something about the very low pay and the poor holiday situation the island education will be in dire straights soon. It will be a close run thing between diminishing population and enough teachers and nurses to maintain the place!

Just as well we are off on leave or I might be moaning too or asking for part time. I am having a lot of fun with my drawing and am finishing off a series 'Views from the golf course' by doing one of the clubhouse. I want to get it done in time to give a set of cards to the Governor before he leaves as he is always going on about the golf course being his spiritual home. I think Dad and I are good for him as we are totally outside all the 'goings on' in government and are two of the very few people who will listen to all his chatter without passing anything on. Maybe we are doing some good here after all!

Now our tickets have arrived I am about to write to some random guy who visited St Helena and joined us on a dolphin trip, to see what he suggests for Easter Island. We received a reply from Richard in Mongolia the other day; he will be having other visitors next summer, but will be able to fit us in for our final leave! We haven't had this leave yet.

Date: 4th September
To: Beth
Subject: Moving house again

Very many apologies for not replying earlier but we do honestly have a very good reason. All your info on your activities with the CHaOS road show sounded great and you obviously thoroughly enjoyed it. I had no idea that you went all the way up to Scotland. You seem to have been working pretty hard as an interior decorator for Tim and Jo as well. We are not quite clear about the river. How far above it is their house? Just thinking of those floods in the West Country that came on the news the other week.

We did actually manage to watch the opening ceremony of the Olympics, which I agree was great as was the closing one. We had a reasonable amount of coverage by DSTV from South Africa and dad did a lot of taping for me so I could catch the stuff that came at odd times besides being able to wizz past the boring talking bits.

The Olympics was in the first week of the holiday and moving was the second. Yes I know 'not again' I hear you say. It has all happened very quickly. Things being as they are here Dad didn't really believe it until we had the keys in our hands. The house is called Cliff Top and it is at the top of Ladder Hill. If you get to the top of the Ladder and then look inland and further along the top of the cliff above Jamestown about 300 yards there we are. It is an imposing double storey house with big verandas upstairs and down. It was originally the officers' mess and it is over 100 years old. It has the most fantastic views. We look out to sea of course and over the whole of James Bay and the Waterfront. Then we can watch everything that goes on in the town 400ft below, besides monitoring all the traffic that goes up Side Path on the other side of the valley. We can see inland almost to Diana's Peak and over to the ridge that leads to Deadwood Plain and Longwood as well as Flagstaff. Brilliant!

The stonewalls of the building are all about two foot thick and there is plenty of space and a very adequate if strange collection of furniture; some of it antique. Much to dad's delight there is a courtyard with three big rooms off it in which he can store all the baggage so we don't have to throw away a single thing - groan! It is about a half hour trek from the kitchen to the loo unless you go to the loo at the other end of the courtyard in which there is also an outside shower. We have heard stories of wild parties in which this enclosed courtyard and the shower seemed to play quite a part but I haven't enquired further. The garden slopes steeply away of course. It was once superb apparently but now is a desert due to the over enthusiastic application of weed killer by AN&RD. So it has been the cardboard box and wrapping routine yet again although unfortunately without the accompaniment of Classic FM this time.

Weather has been cold and wet with lots of wind and a fine swirling mist. This has meant that we have had to abort golf at least twice in the last 10 days but I did get a game in last Wednesday. Dad is planning to join the Environment group for an assault on Lot tomorrow: the last of the official Post Box walks for which he can get a stamp.

We know that you will tell us when there is progress over work. We are thinking of you and are absolutely sure you are doing the right thing and that you will get the right job in the end. If you go to an Agency make sure that you read the small print.

Date: 10th September
To: Jon and Chinatsu
Subject: Wedding bells – Saint style

I hardly dare write the next bit of news for fear that the mention of another member of the family moving into a new house might send you both into a serious spasm, with terminal consequences. But that is what we have done – to the top of Ladder Hill.

The other thing of note is that we were invited to a St Helena wedding last week end (which didn't help the packing effort but was much more fun). The wedding ceremony was rather subdued without the exciting 'starting a new life' feel. This might just be due to the fact that the bridegroom had been married before and the bride had her 5 year old daughter as a bridesmaid (all very St Helenian). There was also a minimal amount of music at the ceremony despite the bride's mum being in the choir.

We trooped out into swirling mist and rain so skipped most of the photos and went across the road to the

Community Centre for drinks and toasting the bride and groom and for a typical island meal. This consisted of fishcakes and pork, plo and curry, black pudding and coleslaw though there was very little tuna! Saints always pull the stops out over food at this sort of event and you really get to see what there is on the island. There always seems to be enough to feed an army.

Being expats it was quite an honour to be invited to this part of the celebrations. As we arrived we made our way, through the pink and red paper flowers, the silver heart-shaped balloons, the curtains of streamers, past the bar and the central table proudly displaying the three cakes (one for the couple and one representing each of the bridesmaids) and up to the B&G. Watched by all, we greeted them and posted our wedding present into the elaborate heart shaped post box nearby (they had asked for financial gifts rather than goods). All this was rather formal and a bit daunting for uninitiated outsiders but the atmosphere gradually relaxed as the main bulk of the guests, of all ages, shapes and sizes, began to arrive for the party. Half the island must have been there in the end (or it felt like it) but that is not surprising as everyone is related, officially or otherwise, to everyone else. The B&G took to the floor and then the two sets of parents after which everyone else could join in and the party took on a more familiar feel.

When things were in full swing I took the opportunity to get the matriarch of one of the main families on the island to explain who various people were and how they were related. This was a mistake. It was so amazingly convoluted. Added to all the formal liaisons and their offspring there were all the informal and casual relationships past and present with all their attendant offspring, and because of the limited number of people on the island these soon began to overlap. My head was spinning in a very short space of time.

We had a good dance and slipped home just before midnight though the party went on to 2am so we were told. In the next several days various people I bumped into commented on each of my dancing partners, which numbers I had sat out and how long we had stayed … nothing an expat does goes unobserved.

Besides all this, my Artistic Company news caused a bit of a slump in shares on the weekly report that stocks hadn't shifted. However futures look a little better as the ship returns in about ten days bringing a bunch of tourists so opening a potential new market. Optimism is high and the latest brand (the landscape cards) is now ready for the launch.

Hope all is well with you and that Danny is wearing himself out enough to give you a good night's sleep.

Date: 3rd October
To: Beth
Subject: Governor departed

Last weekend was the final one for the governor so it was golf on Saturday morning followed by farewell drinks and 'eats' organised the Financial Secretary – a very refreshing and dynamic expat woman – at the Paradise Club in Longwood. Then home to prepare for the evening when I had a dinner party for the Governor and wife and four others, here in the new house. I had had a panic the day before when I saw the lamb leg that I had been saving in the freezer finally unwrapped and unfrozen - it was actually a shoulder and of the African 'chicken chop' variety ie no easily recognisable cut and far more bone than meat!! Still we survived. Everyone seemed genuinely complimentary and I was sent some flowers the next day.

Governor and wife finally left on Wednesday. Probably to the relief of everyone all round as she couldn't get away soon enough and he couldn't bear to leave. He was trying to get everything done before he left and to organise the future as well. His final leave taking was a walk along the waterfront in a very casual shirt and a pair of shorts, shaking hands with the few of us waiting around. This was much disapproved of by many. It was thought that he should have left with more formality.

It has been quite an insight into a whole different area of life in these last few months - interesting but I am not sorry it is over - so many power games and back biting and towards the end the governor wasn't always too well.

Now it is all sights on our travel plans. The school has fixed up for the new supply teacher (wife of the new expat teacher at Prince Andrews) to teach my lessons for me. The fact that she has never taught primary until now but has taught English to adults doesn't seem to have put them off asking her to do all my science! She is a lovely lady but so much for having specialist teachers!

PS. I did the best ever (for me) golf score this Saturday. Whether this has any thing to do with the fact that this was the first Saturday for months that I have not played with the governor I am not sure - but it just may have - he wouldn't ever stop talking!

Date: 4th October
To: Rosemary
Subject: Good Intentions

All my good intentions of writing lots of e-mails in the holidays and keeping up thereafter seem to have faded all too quickly. On a positive note we have had a couple of sermons by the young, fairly recently ordained priest and he has been very good. He gave one extremely challenging one about priorities and choices and that eventually you should face up to the choice of God or what you hold most dear even if the vast majority of us are never required to act on it. Brought me to tears - but also made me wonder about the structure of services that means that one never has time to sit and think and work something through after a sermon because it is up and on with the next hymn. I guess one just has to save it for later.

We are now looking forward to all our plans for our leave. We set off in just under 3 weeks time first stop South Africa next stop Australia etc. Oh yes - please can you tell us about services around Christmas. I am sure that, unlike here, they have already been sorted. What is planned for the Sunday before Christmas? Carol Service? Will you be having the Crib service on Christmas Eve? We are trying to sort out where to be when and of course want to fit in a service or two. Doesn't seem so long now and I am getting quite excited already - a year in this place without a break is more than enough!

Date: 11th October
To: Beth
Subject: Naked Concern

Does anyone know where my clothes are? No that does not mean that I am running round naked (especially in the present distinctly chilly and windy weather) nor has your father hidden them to spice up our life on this island - was that 'oh yuk' I heard you say? No - the problem is that I can't remember what I did with the case of winter wear that you looked after last time. Have you still got it?

Very many thanks for your e-mail today, a lovely long one with lots of news and a reasonably positive tone from you as well. As for 'teaching agencies' you are being very sensible and I guess it is just a case of keep on going frustrating though it is. It is the first time I have been tempted to wish some poor soul had a problem and had to drop out of school (preferably a good one!).

As for life here, there is some speculation over the arrival of the new governor next Friday and the fact that a film crew from a well-known South African TV programme is coming on the same ship. There is also endless talk about the possible new constitution and a new government system and other really exciting things that support my feeling that it is high time we took a break.

Must go and plan more of our visit in the south of Chile. So far every time we communicate with this little airline they have a different version of their flight plans - very much a 'pedal your own' outfit as far as I can see.

Having just looked at the beginning of this letter what a pity it isn't a fax to you at boarding school so I could embarrass the secretary and you in one go.

Date: 18th October
To: Jon and Chinatsu
Subject: The new governor and cyberspace

Things are a bit hectic when the post comes in especially when we get a bumper load. Thank you for the photos of Danny when he was at Chessington. I don't know if I remembered to thank you for them and say how great he looks. I am really looking forward to seeing all the improvements to your house. I must say I wouldn't mind seeing our own downstairs shower room with all its improvements as well as the new garden fence, but I guess we will have to wait until the end of our contract.

Last week we had the arrival of the new governor and the Education dept. agreed to let the schools off for half a day so that children could join the various parts of the parade and watch the official 'signing in' as it were. So children, most wearing the school colours, were rounded up at school and loaded in to the island's fleet of minibuses. The buses then ran relays to get everyone down in to the town square. Crowds gathered while the police, scouts, guides and others assembled in their matching formations. All those of importance and some aspiring to significance found places on the platform outside the courthouse opposite St James' church in the square. I wonder how many similar ceremonies and celebrations have been witnessed by that solid, impartial edifice in the past centuries.

The be-flagged Bentley duly arrived bearing the next in line to carry on his shoulders the responsibilities of this tiny dependent outpost. Some Saints, for whom this was a regular spectacle, were disappointed that this time the white suit and helmet with feathers were not on show! Swearing in completed and speeches delivered, the dignitaries and favoured ones went off for 'eats' and everyone else went about their business or returned home.

The last couple of weeks has been a flurry or perhaps that is a whirlwind of cyberspace activity - is there any wind in cyberspace?? We had our air tickets some time ago but now it was time to start booking hotels and cars and apartments and tickets for the Sydney Opera House. How strange that one is able to look at seating plans and book tickets for a ballet in Australia from a tiny island in the middle of the Atlantic. It has been quite fun although a little frustrating occasionally.

Now it is down to working out the absolute minimum of clothes etc with which we can travel. This, as you can imagine, has resulted in two rather different conclusions. You will sympathise with me Chinatsu when I say that it is much easier for men than women - all they need are two sets of shirt/trousers/underwear, a sweater and a coat with possibly two pairs of shoes. But what about we women? We are going from the hot tropics to near the Antarctic, trekking in the mountains and visiting the Opera House and he tells me I can have half a modest suitcase and some hand luggage!

Date:19th October
To: Beth
Subject: We're off

Just to say my e-mail is taking a break as are we! Hurray. We will try the odd blog to let you know how we are doing - if we can. After all if this place has a system of communications the ones we are going to must have – mustn't they?!........

****

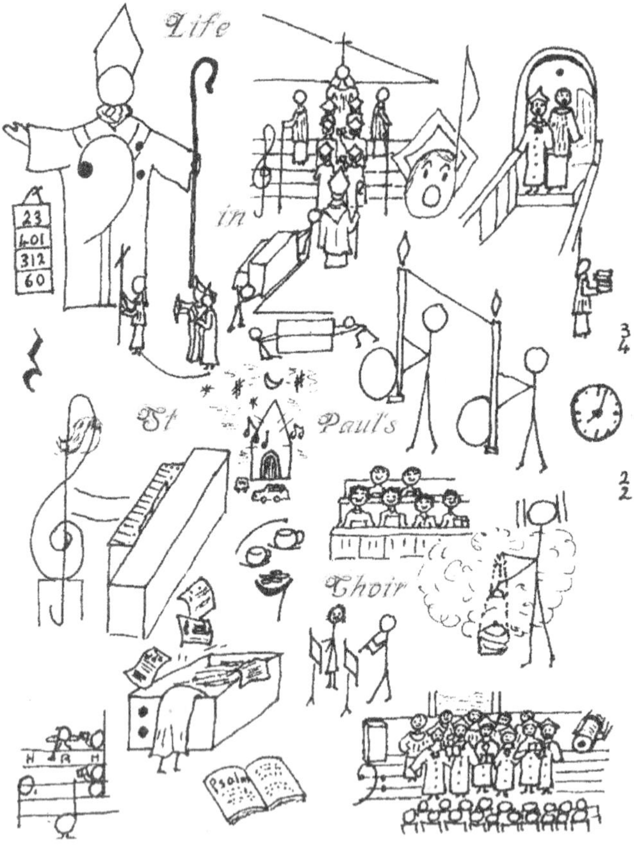
Life
in
St
Paul's
Choir
23
401
312
60
Psalm

PART FOUR
Date: 23rd January 2005
To: Beth
Subject: Once more into exile dear friends

We hit the ground running on our return as it was Burns' Night at Ann's Place and the captain had e-mailed ahead to get us tickets. So there we were on our first evening back, dressed up in all our finery and talking to a haggis. Well some Scottish chap talked to it but it didn't reply, so there was obviously a communication problem. The bishop presided and the governor gave the Burns' speech. It was a good chance to see everyone and catch up on general gossip.

Talking of communications, Dad is presently being rudely reminded that we are back in St Helena and not in an internet cafe in Sydney or Ushuaia or even Easter Island. He is having the greatest difficulty getting connected.

It was rather a ponderous journey back on the ship - seven days at sea rather than five does make it all drag out a bit especially as they turned one engine off a couple of times because we were too far ahead of schedule!! Psychologically that really doesn't work. But it was a good trip and I read three whole books. We made friends with a couple of lovely chaps on our table at dinner. Both six feet, in their late sixties, well educated and well travelled. One loves classical music, especially opera, and the other loves steam trains. They obviously both enjoy good food and good wine and have the figures to prove it. They have been together for at least 30 years!! We also had a very neat, dapper little chap who was a retired BA airline pilot who had flown 747s. Despite having been to all the world's main airports many times he doesn't seem to have really managed to get very far out and about, but he does have a boat for fishing out in the Seychelles.

I gather that there has been a certain amount of

anguish and upset as there was an almighty mix up with the post this Christmas and it appears that nearly all of it went to South America - to Asunción in Paraguay and Georgetown in Guyana! The PO did give an official apology. I presume the post finally came on this last ship which came in from Ascension yesterday and went out today.

It has been incredibly hot and dry the last few weeks apparently, and there have been water restrictions at Longwood. We have been OK at Cliff Top since we arrived back. Richard and I have managed to play a couple of rounds of golf already. The ground is so incredibly dry that this has done my long game a world of good as the ball just keeps on going. However it has made the greens more unpredictable than ever.

I shall go into the education office tomorrow and discuss my return. I can't say I am anxious to rush in to school especially as there have been changes. How lovely that you are finally settled in a proper job and a proper school. I hope it continues to go well though I guess the kids might start testing you now they are used to you.

Date: 6th February
To: Beth
Subject: Counting blessings

I am either going to have to do this all by looking only at the keyboard or at the screen as doing both makes me dizzy at the moment. I seemed to lose my balance on Tuesday evening along with having a bit of a throat and a stuffy nose and it has taken me a while to get back on even keel as it were! Talking of even keel another yacht sailed into the bay this afternoon in glorious sunny weather and a following wind. Apparently people deliver yachts for a living so I am told - what a life.

Where was I - oh yes - so lying dizzily on my bed I thought I had better count my blessings since we returned. Having got over a bad bout of home sickness for the family the positive things are; that I have done three good scores in golf in a row; the weather has been amazingly hot and sunny; we had an enjoyable swim at the pool last Friday; the sea looks a fantastic azure blue (like you see on those impossible calendar pictures of Tahiti); since I did the work last year my lessons take very little planning at the moment and, so far, the bishop has been unusually benign and low key - even when we had a choir practice with him for Jack's ordination.

On the other hand - the teacher who was supposed to be taking my lessons had a row with the Head after two weeks so up and left and odd people have been filling in ever since, and there is still no fruit and veg on the island. Well it is extremely difficult to find as there was some upset with one of the two main shops and so now only one shop is importing and hasn't yet upped the quantities! I have four lemons, two aubergines, half a dozen tomatoes and a carrot in the fridge at the moment. Dad is due to bring back stuff from the market today so we might have a cabbage, some onions and even some passion fruit, which are in season, if we are lucky. That was last Friday and it is now Sunday. Dad did have a little fruit and veg so now a wee cauliflower has been added to the store.

Latest update on the yachts is that two have left and another two have arrived. I watched one as she sailed away towards Ascension Island and after an hour she hadn't gone very far but already looked so small and insignificant in a great big ocean.

Date: 21st February
To: Rosemary
Subject: Cooking and rockfalls

There has been a little bit of excitement for us this week at least by St Helena standards. First the dreaded Valentine's Day seems to have come round again. Now I don't mind Valentine's Day stuff in itself but this was for primary school children and had been inextricably muddled with a Christian assembly. Talk about getting at least two of the four loves confused if not all four. I spent the time in the lab until the last contestants for the Master and Miss V competition had tottered away! Over two hours later everyone finally filed out of the hall and adults came down to have 'eats and drinks' in the Homecraft room, I joined them as I didn't disagree with 'eats'!

Then at 12:00 I suggested that we have a one hour lesson and a slightly shortened lunch hour just to rescue something from the morning. You should have seen the looks on the teachers' faces – total incomprehension and then, despite having just guzzled tea and buns, the teachers said, ' but we haven't had time to eat and we shall be too hungry if we have to wait until 1:00pm'. So we had classes for 20 mins and then.... lunch. I still can't get used to the importance of food in this place.

On a more positive note, after school on Tuesday we had practical fire fighting training and were allowed to get our hands on the fire extinguishers and put out fires lit down on the playing field. It was great fun especially as the woodwork teacher lost control of the powder extinguisher and managed to cover the Head in clouds of the stuff. Whoops!

Thursday was the day of the great veg scramble followed the next day by the great fruit scramble. The ship had come in on Tuesday night. On Friday morning there were apparently about 60 people lined up outside Spar at opening time in order to get their hands on some fruit - it has been that bad this last few weeks - since we got back in fact - with no potatoes, no onions and no fruit. So, on second thoughts perhaps the emphasis on food is justified. Richard managed to get us quite a good selection later in the day, which was nice as we had the visiting judge and her colleague for supper in the evening. I had travelled with them when I first arrived and they were coming to do some training with the magistrates. This was a visit for more training.

Saturday Richard and I went to a cooking demonstration – I know – me and cooking! We managed to slip in a few holes of golf first and then went to one of the more impressive houses on the island set in its own valley and looking straight out to sea. This was for a demonstration by somebody's cousin (a Saint but now a chef in Vancouver). A variety of sushi and then some very nice tuna wrapped in wafers of potato, followed by chocolate mousse and crème anglaise - it was good. It was done partly as a fund-raiser for The League of Friends of the Hospital and partly just to enjoy the food. But I still don't think that cooking is fun.

Now the rockfall. A week ago the experts decided that, once again, there were some unsafe rocks on the slopes above Jamestown and so closed most of the town and evacuated it whilst they did a controlled rockfall. I watched some of it from our advantage point across the valley and the men just looked like ants crawling across the rock face on the opposite side. It took all day and unfortunately resulted in a not so controlled 3 ton rock rolling down on to Ann's Place (one of the two eating places in town) smashing through the wall and landing on her bed in the living quarters at the back. It was all rather traumatic. She of course is rather upset and there will be a great deal of work to do to get everything repaired and up and running again.

Meanwhile everyone is wondering what to do about lunch in town!!

The weather has been fantastically hot and sunny with the sea fairly calm and so clear that we can see the old wreck from World War II below the surface and in the middle of the bay. There are some good points about still being here.

Date: 27th February
To: Olly and Beth
Subject: Ships and sirens

Olly - I've been trying to install the SP3 which you gave me, but without success so far - can you help?

Beth - have you seen the magazine 'Teaching and Learning' incorporating Literacy and Learning and Primary Maths and Science? Issue 10 dated Sept/Oct has lots of lovely stuff about World War II.

This was a hot week with dozens of yachts in and out of the harbour. I do a survey when I get up, and report to dad things like, 'another 'cat' has come in since yesterday' or 'there's one missing, oh, there it is halfway to the horizon'. A cruise ship came in mid-week, but as neither of us was around town we didn't see anything of them. I gather it left behind in the hospital a female member of staff with some medical problem which could not be resolved in a day.

Early on Saturday morning there were sirens ringing in the air, then, when we tried to go to golf up Constitution Hill (behind the hospital) we found it closed off. Apparently someone had died in his car on that road whilst taking the international operator at the Briars Communications Centre home from work: the passenger was shocked and injured, but not fatally.

We're planning to meet up with Jon in Japan in mid-August, just after he attends a residential course there to do

with his Sheffield Japanese studies. We've booked our final passage on the ship from SH on 1st August, and aim to be home by mid-September. They are re-introducing RMS trips to the UK in October, so we shall probably leave our goods and car to come direct, arriving at the end of that month.
Love Dad

Date: 3rd March
To: Joy
Subject: Comings and goings

Richard is still exploring all the possibilities for not coming straight home! We have it in mind to go via Japan since Chinatsu plus bump and Daniel will be there and probably Jon as well. We are also both quite keen to visit China and then we might as well go to Mongolia where my friend is the Ambassador. I think we have more or less given up the idea of the trans-Siberian railway (too much hassle with tickets, visas and sundry other things especially from here) so might go back via Vancouver but definitely missing USA. Who wants to go there at the moment?

Meanwhile back here we have an American ship visiting. We can see the ship all lit up at night from our clifftop eyrie. Our own ship is just about to leave Cape Town to return here via Luderitz and Walvis Bay in Namibia. We have heard that they might have to stay in Walvis Bay for 30 hours or so as the ship with containers, which are from UK and bound for St Helena, has been delayed! I remember we went ashore in Walvis Bay for an hour when we were last there and after 10 mins looking round the town were wondering what else to do. Mind you Luderitz is worse – that takes less than 5! Andrew Weir are exploring possibilities of picking up freight traffic I think.

At present we have clear skies, comfortable SE breezes and brilliant sunshine, and we have half term next week. Not making you jealous or anything. Hope all well in the village and at church.

Date: 13th March
To: Tim and Jo
Subject: Elevation

Congratulations Tim, on your elevation to high office - does one put PCC after one's name to go with all the other letters? Seriously I think it is a good thing and you will enjoy it as long as things actually get decided and done, unlike almost any committee in this place. Talking without commitment and action seems to be the name of the game here. We have a DFID team (of two) at the moment but they need to be out at least a month to see how things really happen (or don't as the case may be) to begin to get the picture. But I guess we are not unique in this.

Tell me - have I got my geography wrong or has Bulgaria moved from Europe to Asia? I thought you were overseeing the Far East in your section. If so, where does a trip to Bulgaria fit in? Still whatever the excuse it sounds as if your trip might be a pleasant interlude. We almost felt as if we were being invaded by the USA this last week as we had not one but two huge US navy container supply ships in the bay at the weekend. As I think I have mentioned they have started to come for Rest & Recuperation. Since we also had the RMS in and a Canadian sail training ship and half a dozen yachts it was positive gridlock in the bay. It is great fun to watch from up here. All these visitors and still nowhere to eat except on Fridays and Saturdays (Donny's and the Coffee Shop) as Ann's is still under repair from the rock fall damage.

My half term seems to have disappeared without me noticing, I reckon I could resign now and I just might get all the things I want to do finished by the time I leave. This includes writing my CV for future excursions into 3rd World poverty-bashing through education and training. Then of course there's been the odd game of golf to return my square eyes to round ones - I wonder if evolution might eventually lead to square eyes especially designed for computers?

Square eyes might not help my singing career, which is about to take another great leap forward. Dad and I have been asked if we would sing at the St Patrick's Day evening entertainment at Plantation House. I know, Dad is Welsh not Irish but this is St Helena. We didn't get invited to the Welsh evening at all, but it is all go - in green - for next Thursday.

Date: 26th March
To: Rosemary
Subject: Enter the 21st century and an Airport

Wow all of a sudden off to the other side of the world and back - great! I am so glad that you took the chance of the holiday. I really loved the little bit of New Zealand that we saw and we certainly hope to try and get back there again if at all possible. Here is one person who is rarely bored at seeing other people's pictures of places they have seen and experienced and I know that you will have thoughts and stories to go with them.

The people here are being hauled into the 21st century according to pronouncements this last week as the Governor announced that St Helena is to get its own airport! - to be built by 2010. Mind you it just might take a little longer than that - changing society I mean. Then again is that a good thing? There are some things that it will be sad to find disappearing but the least attractive elements of modern society are insidiously creeping in and changing life anyway.

It has been a fascinating (and sometimes frustrating) experience to be in such a small community on such a small island, and so isolated and I am glad we have done it but at the same time I shall be more than ready to leave when the time comes. Richard is busy working on the final trip home, which starts on 1st August.

Meanwhile Richard and I were invited to sing as a duet at Plantation to an audience of over 80. The governor was having a St Patrick's night 'do' and asked a friend to get some people together to provide the entertainment. We sang a couple of Irish songs and were accompanied by a fiddle. They went well and someone in the audience wolf whistled along with the clapping at the end, which was rather fun. This was early in the evening before most people had got too far through the free drinks!! It is also possible that we might hear ourselves on the radio as the radio people were there since it was their amplification equipment that was being used. Such giddy heights, it will be a request to make a CD soon.

Mind you on Palm Sunday we had been in the cathedral choir singing 'The Cross of Christ' and that keeps things in perspective! To be fair it really wasn't too bad as long as one wasn't looking for strict timing or dotted notes or anything held longer than two beats. The rest of the sops expire after that and tend to leave me somewhat exposed if we are supposed to hold for 4 - or horrors - 6 beats. That is if the organist doesn't go shooting on regardless because she is singing along with the sops and can't hold the notes either, especially when playing at the same time.

Richard and I will be going to the Salvation Army sunrise service on the cliff top below our house, and then a Eucharist at 9:30 down in Jamestown on Easter Day.

Date: 3rd April
To: Beth
Subject: Submarines

I am going in fear and trepidation - we seem to have invited 60-odd people to a party on the 24th and I am freaking out about the food. However, I am going to see Irene at Harris' Guest House tomorrow so perhaps I shall feel better then - perhaps.

Looking back at Easter - it wasn't too bad in fact it was quite nice. We went to the Maundy Thursday service down in Jamestown, the Good Friday Hour at the cathedral, the Salvation Army sunrise service at the top of Jacob's Ladder (with about 30 people including the band), then the main Easter service with hymns down at St James in town. Dad and I spent most of the rest of the weekend just relaxing – quite exhausting being holy!

There was fun in town on Friday. We have a second radio station that has been going about 4 or 5 months and run by a couple of bright young women. It was set up as a counter to Radio St Helena which is seen as a mouth piece for the government. The new station put out a news item saying that there was an American submarine in the bay but the governor had asked please would people not go and look at it as it was top secret.

Well - the RMS had come in early that morning and as soon as the announcement about the submarine was made all the workers down at the wharf downed tools and refused to continue ferrying the cargo from ship to shore as it was deemed unsafe because of the submarine. Apparently there was chaos, and it took a little while to sort out that it was an April Fool by the radio station, and to get the chaps back to work unloading again. Not sure what was said to the two girls!

I still have four weeks' full time teaching so had better go and sort something out with a semblance of enthusiasm

Date: 10th April
To: Jon and Chinatsu
Subject: Scary future

Things seem to be moving very quickly now don't they? All those decisions about what should go to Japan, what should stay and what should be got rid of. Has Danny sensed the imminent changes yet or will that come when his stuff has to be packed? Still an exciting new chapter just opening, even if some areas are uncertain.

I have been sent away from the kitchen and told to get on with my e-mails whilst Dad does some cooking - has my birthday come early! Well in a way yes - since the cooking referred to is for 'the party' – my 60th'. I am trying to be very sensible and positive and at least not mind the planning and cooking even if 'enjoy' might be stretching it a bit. Dad has promised to help as mentioned. In many ways with something like this, it is not the cooking but the concern about whether we have enough. A lovely Saint lady phoned the other day and offered to make the cake for us. We hadn't even got round to asking who 'does' cakes on the island, so that was nice and she is known to be a great cook. I am going to make a couple of quiches this afternoon to pop in the freezer. Then I shall try and do the odd thing in the evenings during this week and next. Mrs Harris is making plo and some desserts and garlic bread so it is gradually coming together.

I have found it difficult to settle since we returned after Christmas but it is not long now and we are planning a good trip home - I am really looking forward to being able to see you all. Dad is doing all the hard slog in respect of planning. Come bedtime - eventually when I can persuade him to end his love affair with the internet - lights out - settle - nearly asleep - voice in the dark 'do you think 4 days would be enough in Mauritius?' - murmur 'yes dear' - nearly asleep again - 'we'll have to overnight in Singapore' - murmur 'yes dear' - very nearly asleep again - 'should we go to UB before or after Beijing?' -threatening growl 'if you don't go to sleep you won't even make it off the island' - sleep. Wake in the morning - 'I think we should stick with UB then Beijing' - 'I'll go get the tea!'

'Scary future' does not only refer to your plans and our travelling but also to the rather more immediate future in that I seem to have agreed to join in the Ladies' Day golf competition next Saturday. I can't imagine what got into me when Daphne phoned and asked if I would like to join but if it is the women only then I guess if I make a real flop of it we can just have a giggle and get on with the 'bring and braii'. I just hope there is someone as green as me there - pun intended now I've written it!

I didn't watch C and C's wedding yesterday as we were up at the old man, John Beadon's 95th birthday yesterday lunchtime after a round of golf (rained off at the 7th hole). Unfortunately the poor chap had to return to hospital in the middle as he was still recovering from a fall the previous week and came over all funny. He had come out for the party against doctor's orders in the first place, but if you can't do what you want at that age what is the point? I realised that he is 35 years older than me. That's quite something. He talks about working in the bank in Malaya in 1935. He even gave Pope John Paul 11 years.

Two weeks full time teaching in school and then I am done with that bit of my career! With luck the kids might be out for athletics practice, or cheerleaders' practice, or the roads are all closed because of the rock-falls set off by the heavy rain we are suddenly experiencing.

Three cruise ships in next week then no more until next season so they say.

Date: 16th April
To: Beth
Subject: Birthday

HAPPY BIRTHDAY!!!

Not entirely sure where you are at the moment, but that doesn't matter with the web, does it? We will be thinking of you wherever you are.

Dad was woken about 0530 yesterday by the sounds of rocks slithering and bouncing and crashing into metal, which turned out to be a rock-fall on to the wharf area, which has damaged the old customs shed. However the rock guards are already busy organising controlled (hopefully) rock-falls in the area of upper Jamestown near the one-way system at the bottom of Ladder Hill. It's the recent heavy rains (end of summer) which have loosened everything.

Date: 20th April
To: Beth
Subject: New career again

Life is going to be very difficult when I retire, as I just won't be able to decide which career move to make. Dad and I have yet another gig this weekend and now the female equivalent of Tiger Woods (can't remember her name) had better watch out for the competition!

Dad and I have been asked to sing at the St George's Day celebration at Plantation House on Saturday evening which should set us up well for the party on Sunday! We are singing 'Greensleeves' but haven't got round to practising yet - must be careful not to be too blasé.

Now, my golfing career! It was a Ladies' Day event and I thoroughly enjoyed it. I wasn't even as nervous as I expected. The weather was very kind being mostly cloudy with occasional sunshine. I proved to be up to the task instead of disgracing myself. The 17 ladies were followed by all the men and there were lots of light-hearted comments in the evening, about how the men had been held up so much on the way round. The first three places were taken by senior Saint ladies who had all been playing for years. Then guess who came in just out of the medals – me!!! From beginner to fourth in a competition in three years, I was definitely chuffed with that. In the evening we all had a BBQ at the club-house and the bank manager, who is leaving next week, paid for the drinks. A good time was had by all.

We have been able to watch the visit of two cruise ships in the last fortnight and over this weekend two Royal navy ships. We had the captains and some officers from the RN ships up to church on Sunday. They were flown in by helicopter. The padre was invited to preach so that was a real bonus. It was quite amusing as he was obviously used to preaching either out in the open on deck or in a big space and so he spoke really loudly. Nice chap to talk to though.

Today we had the primary schools' athletics day, which was close to a disaster as there was a considerable amount of rain. The rain came over in waves and resulted in everyone crowding up the terrace steps and squashing like damp, steaming aliens into the spectator sheds at the top. When it stopped they all spilled out again and onto the muddy grass. The event kicked off an hour late as there was trouble with the music for one of the First School cheer leader routines - aah, and the electricity went off twice which rather held up the cooking of burgers and chips for singularly unhealthy lunches.

As usual, the non-competitors were far more interested in food and spotting their friends and relatives amongst the senior school students who appeared at break times! Never mind, we completed most of the events and loaded the kids on the buses for home more or less on time. I am fairly tired but no doubt will buck up when we go down to a sponsored scrabble competition in town, which is the way Dad has decided he wants to celebrate his birthday.

Date: 29th April
To: Tim and Jo
Subject: 60 and all

Many thanks for your e-mail and birthday wishes. We seem to have been thinking and planning for the party for about a month or so and the lists began to litter my desk. There were the hours I spent designing the invitation card: the cooking sessions spent by each of us (usually separately to maintain good marital relations): the collection of crockery and cutlery by dad from the TEC and collection of extra tables and chairs from school by both of us: the ordering of some food (especially the typical Saint dishes) from two different people in town who actually like doing that sort of thing: the buying of drinks and hiring of glasses by dad. Oh yes Dad also typed out a list of all (well most) of the significant moments in my 60 years to be displayed on fluorescent cards in the entrance hall. I have had quite a time in quite number of countries when you look at it like that! We were home at a reasonable time after nipping up to sing at Plantation House so despite having last minute things to do we didn't get to bed too late.

      The day dawned, and it was blowing great guns which up here in Cliff Top is very impressive. Some food was delivered here and some collected from town. One teacher arrived at 12:30pm as that was the best she could do for transport especially on a Sunday. Her husband was working on the wharf as the ship had come in earlier in the day. There really was very little for her to do to help except slice the tomatoes and lay them out. By the way these made as much impression as any of the other food as far as I can gather as 'tomatoes is finished' at the moment so it seems. I've just been collecting a few a week and forgetting to use them.

Then just before 1pm when people started to flock in, I had a phonecall from UK - it was Simon with greetings from him and then Grandpop had a chat. He sounds a lot older now but remarkably with it. Then it was just dish out the food and enjoy the party. Of course here you don't worry about people not having anyone to talk to since even though they covered different parts of my life here - school, Education head office, cathedral choir, museum, golf and expat general - everyone is related or knows everyone else anyway. I found a whole lot of teachers and choir ladies tucked round a table at the end of the house having a whale of a time. There were about 50 people altogether of whom about a dozen were expat.

In the middle of the party when everyone was deep into the icecream and flan etc we could see the police putting up a barrier at the top of Ladder Hill. The phone started ringing and messages were flying! Apparently there had been yet another rock-fall. This time it was only light but the rock guards had to go out and assess the area and while this went on access up our side of the valley from town was cut off. Luckily almost all our guests were here, although arrangements for getting home were made more complicated.

Around 3:30 we had the grand cake cutting etc and tea and coffee. Mabel gave me the magnificent fruitcake with its intricate covering of icing as my present. Now that was someone who really understands me (a lovely Saint lady whom I have only recently got to know). People then gradually began to drift away and they had all gone by 5:30. Dad and I sat down to have a drink and something to eat ourselves when........... up pop Jill and Bill, the ones who run the coffee shop. They had only just finished in town having promised to fill in at the new radio station after they closed the shop while the presenter popped out for a while - something to do with the rock-fall!! So we found them a beer or two or three and some plo and chilli con carne and I started opening my presents!

It took me three days to finish opening everyone's presents as they all arrived at the same time so I couldn't do it there and then. Apart from three St Helena peg-bags and two St Helena aprons I have a remarkable variety of things some of which are lace and crochet items made by the old ladies of the island. I was delighted. (NO I am not now old enough to join them.) There were also a couple of beautiful items made from local wood by local craftsmen. I spent some of yesterday drawing and scanning the 'thank you' card. That was fun as I am discovering more and more to do with the scanner and my pictures. Dad says there is birthday mail in the Bag but it seems to have missed this last ship, which came in on Sunday. Maybe it will be in the bag on return from Ascension tomorrow.

Your holiday plans sound excellent. I guess I wouldn't recognise many of the places we went to in Turkey since it was forty years ago, except perhaps one or two out in the real country. We did get to the cave churches at Göreme, though perhaps even those have been commercialised by now.

It seems that we have to go out to a Teachers' Association BBQ tonight which I don't really fancy but I guess we can show our faces then creep out.

Date: 6th May
To: Rosemary
Subject: Changes

We are just coming to the end of our two week holiday at the end of the second term - we only took a couple of days off in the middle of term for Easter as it was so early this year. I ended with a flourish in that my birthday was on the Sunday after the end of term and here on the island everyone makes a big deal of reaching 60 (and promptly retiring - the very next day!!!). We decided that it would be an ideal opportunity to invite all our friends from various areas of our life on the island and have a big celebration in this rather unusual house with its commanding location.

    I told school that I wanted a little time before we left, so would do two days a week to help the year sixes as they come up to their exams and also the year fives. The idea is that I manage a bit of drawing and writing, as well as helping out at the museum before I start on the sorting and packing for our departure on 1st August.

    Our Jon has decided that the ethics, such as they are, of the financial world are not for him, neither is the pattern of being away from home from 7am to 7pm so Chinatsu and he have bought a house near her family in Japan. Chinatsu has returned to Japan with Danny and Jon will follow as soon as he has sold the house here! He is in the middle of a university course in Japanese Translation and hopes to become a freelance translator when he's finished, meanwhile finding anything he can to fill in. It means their life is very uncertain for a while but it is the right thing. I was surprised he lasted in the world of high finance as long as he did. These changes mean that we have slightly reorganised our trip home and will be visiting Jon and Chinatsu in Japan before going off to Mongolia.

Date: 16th May
To: Beth
Subject: Part time – huh!

Yes well - the first day that I have off whilst everyone else is at school lasted until about 10:30am. I was just settling down to compile another radio programme and the telephone goes. It is the Science Adviser who is teaching at Prince Andrew school but has agreed to do the year 4s at St Paul's, asking if I have any notes for the lessons she is teaching in the next 5 minutes? This was not the idea. I gave her ideas there and then and had to go up to school with the rest of the notes later in the day.

I did the radio programme and then recorded it next day on my own as dad was busy with exams and teaching. In the evening we had the Nurses' Ball which is rather a grand title for the event. It was a pleasant evening at the Consulate Hotel but not very well attended. Not many of the nurses themselves came and other people bought tickets but did not turn up in support. Rather a typical response I am afraid. Friday I was at school officially. Saturday was golf and then a sort of 'wake' at the attorney general's house in memory of the old man we used to visit every other Saturday lunchtime. John died as a result of the fall he had taken getting out of a land rover.

Back home and I had to make a pudding and a salad. I know - food again. Since I didn't exactly have much in the way of ingredients I made a variation of a bean salad with kidney beans and corn and then a fruit salad with a tin of peaches and some tired grapes and a couple of apples which are plentiful just for once. Note my enthusiasm - huh! We took my creations off to Blue Hill Community centre as the League of Friends was having a BBQ there.

Sunday Whitsun service at which the bishop was quite reasonable, then after lunch a visit down to Donny's to greet all the walkers who had spent the day walking from Sandy Bay Beach on the south side of the island, over the shoulder of Diana's Peak and down to the Waterfront on the north! Remember your walk from the wharf steps up to the Peak?

Must write to the Martins now and thank them for their Christmas card which the lady in Longwood supermarket gave me the other day (ie 10th May). I know there was a mess up with Christmas post this year but goodness knows how long it has been up in Longwood.

Date: 17th May
To: Jon
Subject: Relays

I have just returned from town and can confirm that The Baton is a metre long, tastefully curvy, coloured metal, stick thing with lots of lights on. If you look into your far distant past you will remember running your little legs off carrying a wooden stick towards another little soul who promptly carried it back to where you had come from. This seemingly futile exercise is called a relay. There is going to be a Commonwealth Games in Melbourne, Australia next year and apparently it has become a tradition (can't remember how many years you have to do something for it to become a tradition) for a baton to be carried from the Q of E to the city where the games are to be held, bearing a message of goodwill and all that stuff.

This year they have excelled themselves and have arranged a relay where the baton will visit every country of the Commonwealth! Mind you if you look at the itinerary there has been a serious lapse in the teaching of geography to the organiser. Maybe the pages fell out of their atlas and they put them back in a different order or they remember the aforementioned race from childhood. The baton is carried/guarded by a beefy Australian policeman and a photographer who refuse to pass it to anyone (at least not for long) so I have heard - is that still a relay?

Sorry the house is taking a while - very frustrating for you.

PS About 3 weeks ago I got a lovely Mothering Sunday card from you! Did I remember to thank you?

Date: 17th May
To: Tim and Jo
Subject: The baton

The ship arrived today with the governor (returning from a governors' conference), a chief justice (coming to judge at the murder trial) and the Commonwealth Baton! The visit of the last has been timed to coincide with St Helena Day. All sorts of jolly activities are organised each year for this day, with most of the island turning out for one event or another. I think I am selling raffle tickets for the 'League of Friends of the Hospital'.

Today however, I was down at the wharf, lining up with all the school children, to greet 'the baton' off the ship. The children then did their cheerleader routines and the baton went up Jacob's Ladder and then back down into town in the charabanc via Ladder Hill Road. The baton will do sundry other things during its stay including a visit to each school to enable it to explain what it is all about!! I know 'it' is a high tec. piece of steel and electronics but the way the island has been talking about it you'd think it was a person.

Dad is making good progress with our return journey. We are now at the stage of looking for and booking places to stay.

Date: 22nd May
To: Jon
Subject: School day memories

Great news about Danny and the nursery school though it makes one sit up to think that he has got to that stage already! I wonder if he will be like Tim was when he went to the nursery school in Malaysia. Rather a determined mind of his own had our Tim. If they put out plasticine for his group to play with for half an hour and he didn't fancy it he just took himself off to the bricks, or even to the next class and settled with those whilst the staff looked bemused and let him. The rest of his playmates duly played with the plasticine for the allotted time!! He was only 3 and you were at home with Amah Grace. Oh yes I think he only got 6 out of 10 for his art work - not much change there then except perhaps with photography!

  We had a glorified fete type activity on Francis Plain on Friday. Nearly half the island seemed to turn up for the parade, the arrival of the baton and then marching, stalls, raffles, competitions and of course the beer tent! as part of the St Helena Day celebrations. I was setting up the stall and selling raffle tickets for the League of Friends (regular WI type I am becoming - help - no, not that!). In the evening we had the rest of our quiz night team round for a drink and an informal meal to celebrate our winning of the said quiz the previous Wednesday. Dad had to do some of the cooking as I only arrived after the guests.

  We have the last of the 'baton' events that I shall be involved in tonight as there is a 'Songs of Praise' at St James church down in the town. Come to think of it I don't know if anyone asked the baton if it was Anglican or even Christian. Just thinking about it - are there many of the Commonwealth countries that do not have a strong element of Christianity in them?

Date: 25th May
To: Rosemary
Subject: An unusual service and the baton!

It is the middle of the week and school term, and here I am at home writing e-mails and contemplating going out to play golf with a friend of mine. It feels very odd. I certainly want to get stuck into something other than golf when I get home. How to find the right thing is concerning me somewhat at the moment, but it is probably best to wait until we get back in mid September.

 I had another read of your e-mail about New Zealand this morning and it really does sound fantastic and very special. I expect it seems rather a long time ago now. Richard is deep into planning our next trip and Mongolia is proving to be quite a challenge! Meanwhile back here at the centre of the universe there has been quite a stir.

 Come last Sunday evening there was the final event for the visit of the Commonwealth Baton -'Songs of Praise' at St James down in town. Our church is truly amazing when it can manifest itself in so many ways - if it hadn't been so cringingly embarrassing it would have been funny and like a scene out of Mr Bean. I will explain. 'Songs of Praise' in honour of the visit of the Commonwealth baton was instigated, as far as I know, by the Ladies' Orchestra headed by Heather, a very competent, lovely lady. They have been practising for weeks. The congregations throughout the island were all invited to join in the evening service at St James, as were the choirs from the cathedral and St Matthew's in Longwood. We arrived in good time as requested, as this was also to be a live radio broadcast.

 The members of the orchestra were all in place between the choir stalls; our choir duly arrived (and there were actually enough books for us all); the radio mikes were up and running and the congregation was gradually filling up the rather large church. The Chief Secretary, his wife and the visiting high court judge were settled in the front row. Seven o'clock arrived ... but no Commonwealth Baton! It had been taken to all the districts on the island and was still somewhere at the top of Ladder Hill! Never mind - the bishop announced that we would begin the service anyway and it would no doubt arrive soon.

So an opening prayer and over to his junior priest (earnest and intelligent) to officiate or is that compere?! the proceedings. The first hymn was announced and the orchestra had just struck up when this priest, dressed in his monk's habit, launched forth loudly into the first verse, ahead of the music and with great gusto (the mike two inches from his face). He then started to wave his hands about energetically and the sleeves of his habit flapped like flags around his bare arms - and so it continued throughout the hymn. Much the same happened in the next hymn. It dawned on more than one of us that perhaps he had had a touch too much sun! Startled, horrified and embarrassed looks gradually spread from Heather to the orchestra members, the choir and a number of the congregation. The lady sitting next to me got up and nipped round to where the radio technicians were and suggested that they turn the monk's mike off during the singing as the people at home wouldn't hear anything else! The Baton, by the way, still hadn't arrived.

We had a reading and a solo, for which we were all commanded to clap, and then it was physical jerks time again. As a result of sufficient glares from Heather, he actually waited for the orchestra this time and we made it to the end almost together. What we hadn't bargained for was the bishop adding his pennyworth. You know 'allellu, allellu, allellu, allelluia praise ye the Lord'? Well - yes you've guessed it - the bishop had the entire congregation, at least half of whom were well over 70, jumping up and down according to the bit they were singing. Not sure how that episode came over on the radio!

Back to our leader who, by the way, had been enjoying a wild knees up. It was now time for him to do his solo. Normally he is an excellent musician with a lovely tenor voice. He started off well and I sat back to enjoy it. However what followed was a crack in the voice, a dodgy falsetto and the apparent need to support himself with the lectern for the last bit. He ended with a modest smile and announced the next hymn. Now it was happy-clappy time during which there were some less than happy searching looks as to the progress of the Baton. Apparently it was now at the top of Jamestown.

Another reading, a few prayers, a duet and the presentation of the 'St Helena Young Person of the Year' award (not sure why that slipped in) and we were on the last hymn. We had sung all 4 verses when the Baton arrived - more or less. There seemed to be some kerfuffle at the west door so the monk called out brightly for us all to sing the first verse again ... and the second, and the third and the fourth. Finally the Baton was making its way down the aisle and what does he do but start us all off for the third time - those of us who were prepared to. Even the Ladies' Orchestra had rebelled by this point.

So at last, Baton in place, hymns sung and prayers said, the bishop started on his thank-you speech. After we had clapped every conceivable person, probably including the cleaners and the resident mynah birds (I wasn't concentrating by then) we were allowed to escape and put that one into the 'one we'll never forget' category of experiences. It transpires that the judge, the bishop and the priest had all been out to the Chief Secretary's house for an excellent Sunday lunch including all the extras that would go with such an occasion!

There's certainly an 'experience' around every corner on this island.

Date: 8th June
To: Jon
Subject: Fancy dress

I went out to the golf course after school yesterday and did my second best score ever. Just thought I'd tell you even if golf isn't quite your thing!! Then last Saturday we went on our final dolphin trip with some old hands and a bunch of newcomers. We saw hundreds of dolphins and at least four different kinds. Even I could see that the bottle nosed were about twice the size of the pan .... something ones! All this science tends to overwhelm one. Not many dolphins were jumping but there were a few impressive efforts and a lovely little teenager who was desperately trying to impress but had some way to go.

  We got back for a late lunch and in time to put the finishing touches to the fancy dress costumes (theme - aliens) for Bill's (of Jill and Bill coffee shop) surprise birthday celebration at Signal House - just below us. Unfortunately Ann of Ann's Place had forgotten to do the food so there was a frantic last minute rush round to the supermarket and instant improvisation and on this island that is quite a challenge. Dad was just delivering chairs and had two packets of frozen samosas thrust in his hands with instructions to get Sue to cook those. Just up my street!

  Never mind it all went off well and they weren't really burnt. I had made a triangular head-dress out of coat hangers wrapped in foil and topped by a demonstration 'eye' from school for Dad; and a cardboard box covered with foil, with a set of giant-sized demonstration teeth jutting out in front and two foil-covered golf ball eyes with dazzling silver eyelashes stuck on top, for me. All that Blue Peter and primary school teacher training had to be good for something. Went down a treat.

Sunday we skived off church and climbed Flagstaff - one of Dad's favourite walks. The next day I put in more extra time for the school as I took a bunch of kids to plant trees in the rocks above the swimming pool - I know sounds odd - why in rocks? It's all this 'environment week' stuff. Hilarious, they referred to Jamestown as being a city - apparently Queen Victoria had declared it as one, so who are we to argue?

Today I have what will probably turn out to be my last dinner party at here at Cliff Top (whew). It is a farewell for the above Jill.

Date: 10th June
To: Beth
Subject: Boiling oil

The ship came in yesterday and it brought the last bit of my birthday - talk about stretching it out. Thank you my love - very nostalgic and thoughtful. In fact a dose of 'Sound of Music' is exactly what I needed after a slightly traumatic dinner party.

The dinner party was for Jill as she is leaving next week and she has been the one who has been here all the time we have and made us welcome at the beginning. I have also played golf with her almost every Saturday that we have both been on the island. The other guests were the usual gang of Jill and Bill (coffee shop), David (lives in Canada - does development type stuff) and Linda (Financial secretary). Interesting folks - three of them being smokers, all good drinkers, occasionally available for philosophical discussion, very genuine, jolly and a good laugh.

I had planned things well in advance ie at least 5 days ahead (you are required to be impressed) and was feeling very relaxed (that's what part-time does for one). I had asked Mabel to make a gateau and she suggested that I do strips of fish in batter on a bed of salad for starter to go with the pork main meal. She even offered to prepare the fish and batter. I had been to town the day before and actually managed to get 3 kinds of veg - wow. Spent all afternoon gently preparing everything and listening to the radio (well one has to do something useful whilst preparing food). I followed what's-her-name - Delia to the letter in making a Spanish Casserole and it all worked beautifully as I had all the ingredients (must try following a proper recipe again sometime). Gateau and fish were duly delivered, dad prepared the table and rooms as usual and the guests arrived.

  Since it was a very pleasant evening, although a little cool, everyone decided to have their first drinks on the downstairs verandah. I had all the starter dishes laid out, the saucepans all full of veg on the top and the casserole in the oven. I put a pan of oil on the stove to heat up for deep-frying and popped out to tell the jolly party on the verandah it wouldn't be long when - bang - the front door shut. Oops it was on a yale - everyone laughed - 'got the key Richard?' someone asked. 'Well as it happens no' was the reply. Big laugh all round 'well we will just have to climb in a window'. All windows locked as the house is very draughty anyway and it was cold. 'Well never mind have another drink and we will think about it!'

  'Actually', I pipe up, 'I think we ought to think about it fairly quickly as there is a pan of hot oil sitting on the stove!' Ahhhh!

  So a tour of the premises was instigated. Unfortunately for this situation our back door opens on to a courtyard completely surrounded by high stone walls and, because of our exposed situation and our Africa experiences, everything is locked and bolted. Hmm. Dad and Linda scrabble around in the dark by the courtyard door to see if she can climb over (she is younger and I have no shoes) but the wall is too high there. Quick conference as, when we get round to the verandah again, there is a distinct smell of hot oil. Nothing for it - better call the fire brigade. Two people are detailed to go further down the hill to phone whilst another two search for another way over the wall.

This time David had got his torch from the car and they are investigating the old urinal in the corner, by the side of the house (which used to be an officers' mess). David manages to heave Bill up high enough for him to get on the top of the wall. Bill then climbs over the roof of the outside toilet and down into the yard. Into the kitchen, grab pan which has not quite caught fire and put it down on table covered with plastic fablon! Open front door to let everyone in. We now had to shout down to the house below to stop them calling the fire brigade. After that everyone needed a drink - and I went off to deep fry the starter!!

Thought the above diversion would cheer you up after a week at school.

P.S. By the way would you believe it but I am sitting here with a disgustingly bright Garfield plaster on my thumb - I have split my nail and Half Tree Hollow SPAR gave me the choice - Garfield or the Simpsons! - they had nothing else in the store.

Date: 18th June
To: Beth
Subject: Soggy

We have had a somewhat quieter week starting with Monday off for the Queen's birthday. Which reminds me perhaps the official birthday should vary according to the season and the different parts of the world. It is daft to have the QBP here in June when we have such a wet and windy month. Maybe I ought to have a word with Her Majesty. The whole thing went off smoothly enough with the marquee this time set up on the side lawn. We are now in a position to talk to lots of people, and recognise a great many faces. However just as the governor began his speech, standing up on a small dais outside, a fine mist blew in. This slowly increased to quite heavy rain. Michael manfully continued with the speech whilst his audience gradually withdrew under the marquee. I was thinking, as he and his notes got soggier and soggier, it was perhaps just as well that he was not wearing the formal feathers after all!

Talking about soggy conditions, we had the wettest of competitions in golf last weekend. It was a Texas Scramble and Gill and I were persuaded to enter. There were 48 people and it all took a long time to get started. Finally when our four went out the wind was howling, the mist was swirling and we could only just make out the first green. By the time we were teeing off for the third we could hardly see a thing. We had a South African visitor who didn't know the course and had to tell him to aim between the trees that were just discernable on the edge of the road, and hope for the best.

Conditions improved slightly as we went down the fourth but then clamped down again and all the while we were getting wetter and colder and the wind increased. We could hardly see where I had hit the ball let alone the visitor who was very good. We finished 9 holes but then called it a day as did a couple of other groups and went off to Gill's for a hot shower and a change. Enough people finished for the prizes to be given out and the curry and rice afterwards was excellent. However since then I have done several good scores so feel quite pleased.

Just remembered - I pandered once more to my demanding public and was interviewed for 20 minutes on the radio! Listened to it next day and it didn't sound too bad at all. I then went down fresh food hunting (it being Thursday) and several people mentioned that they had heard it - odd feeling that. It came about because I had been chatting to Gary during the recording of our music programme, about all the countries we had worked in, and he asked if could he interview me.

Date: 2nd July
To: Tim and Jo
Subject: Turkey and prison

Great to hear how the building project is working out. The holiday in Turkey sounds good too and I know exactly what you mean about feeling as if you were back in time. I remember when Anne and I hitched there as university students and the first time I saw a family threshing corn with a donkey pulling a heavy wooden board round and round on the threshing floor, and another man winnowing with a wooden fork with the chaff blowing in the wind. Talk about New Testament times. We also went to the large arena at Ephesus and stood there imaging the crowds roaring, 'great is Diana of the Ephesians'. As you say – fantastic stuff.

Since the coffee shop has closed for the winter we don't seem to see so many people. The last major fuss was all to do with the trial and everyone's dissatisfaction with the sentencing. Only 'four years' for manslaughter in a murder case involving a well-known, long-standing feud and a considerable amount of alcohol, did not go down at all well. At the same time the judge said that he hoped this would be a deterrent to people who drink too much. This was not exactly convincing when the same judge had previously put two people in jail for six years for marijuana abuse. A couple of the top silks from London came out for the case.

We have been entertained a couple of times at farewell dinners and last night there was a St Andrew's ceildhi at the Consulate Hotel, which was great fun. There was plenty of real Scottish country dancing to be had, besides haggis and stovies.

Date: 4th July
To: Beth
Subject: Bumbling

You sound amazingly cheerful instead of worn out for three weeks from the end of term! My lot are doing their SATs science tomorrow, which I am going to supervise. Mind you whether they will have caught up on sleep after being glued to late night films and hanging round the Consulate at all hours for a week of half term I don't know - it is a bit of a gamble.

We have had a couple of farewells already. The first was the League of Friends who put on a great supper at Gay's house out at Blue Hill. It is a beautiful house that has been extended and improved with masses of wood panelling and so on. In the middle of last week there was the school farewell for me at Harris' Guest House. It was very pleasant and people were fairly relaxed and chatty which was a relief as people are often silent and awkward at these affairs. They gave me a big blue bag with a nice design of St Helena on it.

Apart from that it is everyone else who is leaving before us so we are saying farewell to them. The bishop has already gone and Father Chris, the dentist, the ex-Chief Secretary, and our friends who used to work in Tajikistan are all going (some on leave and some for good) this week. It is just as well we have some Saint friends. I played golf with a Saint today and we did 18 holes!! It seems very funny doing that first thing on a Monday morning. Apart from golf I have a target to pack at least one box every day and preferably two.

Date: 15th July
To: Rosemary
Subject: Packing and printing

I am down to the last two weeks now and the dining room is full of cardboard boxes. I have just been doing a couple a day though I expect that will increase now. For some of the rest of the time, apart from supervising and then marking the SATs science tests, I have been commissioned, as it were, to design some cards.

The League of Friends has asked if I could design a Christmas card or two! It happens I was just in the mood and so have been having great fun and have also been exploring more and more things that one can do with the scanner programme. I've done the basic drawing, scanned it then added airbrushing, oil painting, touching up, spotlighting and various other things including adding bubbles which cleverly reflect bits of the basic picture. When I have done enough of that I get up and pack another box. It is keeping me occupied if not exactly intellectually stimulated.

It is very odd no longer working but not 'on holiday' - in fact it is quite disorientating. All my life everything has always revolved round going to school/work on Monday to Friday and then weekends with church on Sunday. Even the days themselves have a pattern but that is all topsy-turvy and fluid now. I find I have to make lists and it is a good thing Richard is often here or I would forget to stop and eat during the day - weird.

We are down to one car after lunchtime today having sold the Peugeot to the Chief of Police. He asked if he could buy it when we left and that was in the first month after we had arrived!! Now Public Works Department have closed the Ladder Hill road, which winds steeply down our side of the valley to town. Apparently cracks have appeared in the road and a chunk of it is liable to collapse under the weight of a lorry or school bus and crash down 400ft into St James church, the prison and sundry other buildings - an awful thought. They first banned all heavy vehicles then decided repairs needed to be done straight away, so the road is now closed to everyone This leaves us with a long haul half way round the island to drive into town for the last few weeks of our stay. We can still walk down - it's the steep climb back up the aforementioned 400 ft to get home that I don't fancy too often.

Jon is flying off to Japan to join Chinatsu and Danny tomorrow but of course we will be seeing them in Japan next month on our way home. Chinatsu is expecting their second in December.

Date: 20th July
To: Jon, Chinatsu, Danny and bump
Subject: Arrivals and Farewells

Lovely to hear from you. I'm glad you survived your trip Jon and you sound very perky. The setting for the house sounds beautiful, is it reasonably cool in the high temperatures you are having? This house is looking a bit of a mess with boxes and packing everywhere but I have done the bulk of it now and we are down to the stage where things need to be packed but we want to use them!

Must tell you about last night. We had been invited to a buffet supper, with a lovely Saint lady called Edith, who lives on Crack Plain. She had invited over a dozen of her relatives (mostly nieces and cousins who are visiting the island) as well as us and we all duly turned up around 7.30pm. She herself had only been in about 20 mins as she had been running the Agricultural Society committee meeting. Well we had drinks and chatted. Then had drinks and chatted some more and in fact we continued in this fashion until 10pm when the food (which was very good) finally arrived! I had warned dad that this had been known to happen before. Still it was a good evening and we met some interesting Saints. Edith has travelled all round the world including all the way across Russia on the Trans- Siberian Railway, on one of her trips.

Please give our best wishes to your family Chinatsu, I bet they like having you around again.

Date: 27th July
To: Beth
Subject: Last this and last that

Don't seem to have heard from you for a while. I appreciate that you are right at the end of term but assume that you have actually finished by now. You are obviously a) flat out exhausted or, b) rushing around doing all the things you have been waiting to do when school stops or, c) off on a quick cheapy, cheapy holiday to the costa del somewhere or deepest darkest Eastern Europe or, d) in the middle of writing one of your terrific tales of your activities or, e) about to get in touch but haven't got round to it yet or, f) your last e-mail just got lost or, g) in hospital and no one's told us!

I am sick to death of packing boxes but hopefully will have finished the last ones today. I think I have packed up and moved house over thirty times by now. The poor chap who comes up to pack the big wooden crates with our boxes has to keep going back to order another one. The latest was 'I don't know if you can send any more we don't seem to have any wood and if we did, we haven't anywhere to store them.' We still aren't sending back as much as we came with. As usual we have sold off many things especially the electrical stuff. In that way it is just like Africa.

I found packing a touch difficult last Monday as one ankle was twisted and the other leg was grazed. As Ladder

Hill has been closed for a week and will be for two more, Dad and I decided to walk down the road to the patronal festival service at St James last Sunday evening. All was well until the last two hundred yards of the Shy Road (a horse shied with an important personage on board in an earlier age), when I twisted my ankle on the edge of an unseen pothole and went flying. I managed to hobble to the church and to do the service but we accepted a lift home.

    It is actually OK now but I decided not to have my last game of golf, which was rather a shame, as I didn't want to get myself into more trouble before our slightly roundabout trip home. Dad has been rushing round all over the place being entertained right, left and centre as people have worked out he is going and they want to have a farewell something - be it lunch, tea, drinks, dinner, assembly! I am invited to some of them as well. We have the Senior Management for Education dinner at Ann's tonight.

    Really must finish this last e-mail so that we can box up this machine that has made such a difference to us. See you when we meet up at Jon's in Japan in a month's time.

Meanwhile, we say farewell to this extraordinary island and its people as we end our contract in exile and head off to glimpse several other very different worlds - Mauritius, Japan, China and Mongolia.

Then HOME!

                 Lots of love
                      Mum

                ****

Post Script

Nine years later, work to build an airport has finally begun and when it is finished, life on the island will never be quite the same again.

Airport - www.sainthelenaaccess.com/news/
Tourism - www.sthelenatourism.com